how to
Make
People
Like
You

how to Make People Like You

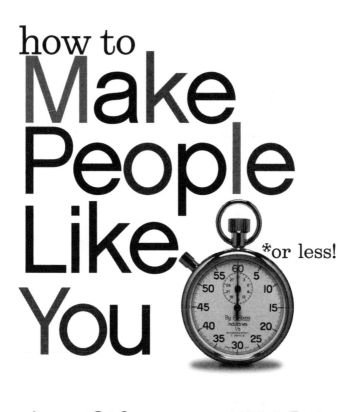

*or less!

in 90 seconds

by Nicholas Boothman

WORKMAN PUBLISHING • NEW YORK

This work was originally published in hardcover in 2000.

Library of Congress Cataloging-in-Publication Data
Boothman, Nicholas
How to make people like you in 90 seconds or less/by Nicholas Boothman.
p. cm.
ISBN 978-0-7611-4946-0
1. Interpersonal communication. 2. Interpersonal relations. I. Title.
BF637.C45 B655 2000

158.2—dc21   00-043236

Workman books are available at special discounts when
purchased in bulk for premiums and sales promotions as well
as for fund-raising or educational use. Special editions or book
excerpts can also be created to specification. For details,
contact the Special Sales Director at the address below.

WORKMAN PUBLISHING COMPANY, INC.
225 Varick Street
New York, NY 10014-4381
workman.com

Manufactured in the United States of America

12 11 10 9 8 7

Whether you like it or not, people decide how they feel about you in the first two seconds of seeing you, or hearing you, if it's on the phone. If they like you, they will unconsciously tend to see the best in you and look for opportunities to say "yes." If they don't like you, the opposite is true.

—Harvard School of Health Sciences

To Wendy, of course.

Acknowledgments

What a glorious piece of synchronicity. My heartfelt thanks go to: My beautiful friend Kerri King, who commanded, "Write it down! Now!" My guardian angel Dorothea Helms, who said, "It's time to get yourself a great publisher." The charismatic book publisher Peter Workman, who brings all his senses to bear on a book and surrounds himself with the finest talent to be found. To his astonishing editor, the late Sally Kovalchick, who blew you away with her ability to inhale a manuscript and exhale a finished book. To Margot Herrera, who took over from Sally and has an uncanny ability to throw everything up in the air and make it land in just the right spot at the right time. And, to my youngest daughter, Pippa Boothman, who turned this book into a 90-minute training course for teens and delivered it to thousands of young people across the continent, as well as contributed her talents to this new edition.

You are all living proof that other people are our greatest resource.

Contents

Preface

The "secret" of success is not very hard to figure out. The better you are at connecting with other people, the better the quality of your life.

I first discovered the secrets of getting along with people during my career as a fashion and advertising photographer. Whether it was working with a single model for a page in *Vogue* or 400 people aboard a ship to promote a Norwegian cruise line, it was obvious that for me photography was more about clicking with people than about clicking with a camera. What's more, it didn't matter if the shoot was taking place in the lobby of the Ritz Hotel in San Francisco or a ramshackle hut on the side of a mountain in Africa: the principles for establishing rapport were universal.

For as long as I can remember, I have found it easy to get along with people. Could it be a gift? Is there such a thing as a natural talent for getting along with people, or is it something we learn along the way? And if it can be learned, can it be taught? I decided to find out.

I knew from 25 years of shooting still photographs for magazines all over the world that attitude and body language are paramount to creating a strong visual impression—magazine ads have less than two seconds to capture the reader's attention. I was also aware that there was a way of using body language and voice tone to make perfect strangers feel comfortable and cooperative. My third realization was that a few well-chosen words could evoke expression, mood and action in almost any subject. With these insights under my belt, I decided to look a little deeper.

Why is it easier to get on with some people than with others? Why can I have an interesting conversation with a person I've just met, while someone else might dismiss that same person as boring or threatening? Clearly, something must be happening on a level beyond our conscious awareness, but what is it?

It was at this point in my quest that I came across the early work of Drs. Richard Bandler and John Grinder at UCLA in a subject with the unwieldy name of Neuro-Linguistic Programming, NLP for short. Many of the things I had been doing intuitively as a photographer, these two men and their colleagues had documented and analyzed as "the art and science of personal excellence." Among a fountain of new insights, they revealed that everyone has a "favorite sense." Find this sense and you have the key to unlock a person's heart and mind.

As my new path became clearer, I set aside my cameras and resolved to focus on how people work on the inside as well as how they look on the outside. Over the next few years, I studied with Dr. Bandler in London and New York and earned a license as a Master Practitioner of NLP. I studied Irresistible Language Patterns in the United States, Canada and England, and delved into everything to do with the brain's part in human connectivity. I worked with actors, comedians and drama teachers in America and storytellers in Africa to adapt improvisational drills into exercises that enhance conversational skills.

Since then I have gone on to give seminars and talks all over the world, working with all kinds of groups and individuals from sales teams to teachers, from leaders of organizations who thought they knew it all to children so shy that people thought they were dim-witted. And one thing became very clear: making people like you in 90 seconds or less is a skill that can be taught to anyone in a natural, easy way.

Over and over I have been told, "Nick, this is amazing. Why don't you write it down?" Well, I listened, and I have. And here it is.

—N.B.

First Contact

Part One

People Power

Connecting with other people brings infinite rewards. And whether it's landing the job, winning the promotion, gaining the sale, charming a new partner, electrifying your audience or passing inspection by future in-laws, if people like you, the welcome mat is out and a connection is yours for the making. Other people are your greatest resource. They give birth to you; they feed you, dress you, provide you with money, make you laugh and cry; they comfort you, heal you, invest your money, service your car and bury you. We can't live without them. We can't even die without them.

Connecting is what our ancestors were doing thousands of years ago when they gathered around the fire to eat woolly mammoth steaks or stitch together the latest animal-hide fashions. It's what we do when we hold quilting bees, golf tournaments, conferences and yard sales; it underlies our cultural rituals from the serious to the frivolous, from weddings and funerals to Barbie Doll conventions and spaghetti-eating contests.

Even the most antisocial of artists and poets who spend long, cranky months painting in a studio or composing in a cubicle off their bedroom are usually hoping that through their creations they will eventually connect with the public. And connection lies at the very heart of those three pillars of our democratic civilization: government, religion and television. Yes, television. Given that you can discuss *The Office* or *Lost* with folks from Berlin to Brisbane, a case must be made for the tube's ability to help people connect all over the globe.

Thousands of people impact all aspects of our lives, be it the weatherman at the TV studio in a neighboring city, or the technician at a phone company across the continent, or the woman in Tobago who picks the mangoes for your fruit salad. Every day, wittingly or unwittingly, we make a myriad of connections with people around the world.

The Benefits of Connecting

Our personal growth and evolution (and the evolution of societies) come about as a result of connecting with our fellow humans, whether as a band of young warriors setting out on a hunt or as a group of co-workers heading out to the local pizzeria after work on Friday. As a species, we are instinctively driven to come together and form groups of friends, associations and communities. Without them, we cannot exist.

Connect and Live Longer

Making connections is what our gray matter does best. It receives information from our senses and processes it by making associations. The brain delights in and learns from these associations. It grows and flourishes when it's making connections.

People do the same thing. It's a scientific fact that people who connect live longer. In their gem of a book, *Keep Your Brain Alive,* Lawrence Katz and Manning Rubin quote studies by the MacArthur Foundation and the International Longevity Center in New York and at the University of Southern California. These studies show that people who stay socially and physically active have longer life spans. This doesn't mean hanging out with the same old crowd and pedaling around on an exercise bike. It means getting out and making new friends.

When you make new connections in the outside world, you make new connections in the inside world—in your brain. This keeps you young and alert. Edward M. Hallowell, in his very savvy book *Connect,* cites the 1979 Alameda County Study by Dr. Lisa Berkman of the Harvard School of Health Sciences. Dr. Berkman and her team carefully looked at 7,000 people, aged 35 to 65, over a period of nine years. Their study concluded that people who lack social and community ties are almost three times more likely to die of medical illness than those who have more extensive contacts. And all this is independent of socioeconomic status and health practices such as smoking, alcoholic beverage consumption, obesity or physical activity!

Connect and Get Cooperation

Other people can also help you take care of your needs and desires. Whatever it is you'd like in this life—romance, a dream job, a ticket to the Rose Bowl—the chances are pretty high that you'll need someone's help to get it. If people like you, they will be disposed to give you their time and their efforts. And the better the quality of rapport you have with them, the higher the level of their cooperation.

Connect and Feel Safe

Connecting is good for the community. After all, a community is the culmination of a lot of connections: common beliefs, achievements, values, interests and geography. Rome wasn't built in a day, and neither was Detroit. Three thousand years ago, in what today we call Rome, Indo-Europeans connected to hunt, survive and generally look out for one another. Three hundred years ago, a French trader turned up to create a safe haven for his fur business; he started making connections and pretty soon Detroit was born.

We have a basic, physical need for other people; there are shared, mutual benefits in a community, so we look out for each other. A connected community provides its members with strength and safety. When we feel strong and safe, we can put our energy into evolving—socially, culturally and spiritually.

Connect and Feel Love

Finally, we benefit from each other emotionally. We are not closed, self-regulating systems, but open loops regulated, disciplined, encouraged, reprimanded, supported and validated by the emotional feedback we receive from others. From time to time, we meet someone who influences our emotions and vital body rhythms in such a pleasurable way that we call it love. Be it through body language, gestures, facial expressions, tone of voice or words alone, other people make our hard times more bearable, our good times much sweeter.

We use the emotional input of other humans as much as we do the air we breathe and the food we eat. Deprive us of emotional and physical contact (a hug and a smile can go a long way), and we will wither and die just as surely as if we were deprived of food. That's why we hear stories of children in orphanages who grow sickly and weak despite being adequately fed and clothed. People with autism may desire emotional and physical contact but can languish because they are hindered by their lack of social skills. And how often have you heard about one spouse in a 50-year marriage

Face to Face

 The Internet has been touted as the ultimate tool for bringing people together into shared communities of interest. And it's true: you can have fun with an ever-expanding network of "friends" on Facebook, and if you're searching for other teddy bear collectors in Toledo or mud wrestlers in Minsk, you'll find them on the Web. For people who are housebound, the Web can also be a godsend.

Still, we have to remember that spending hours in front of a screen, typing into cyberspace, is a poor substitute for the full spectrum of experience offered by face-to-face time with another person. You might well meet someone on Match.com who interests you romantically, but would you agree to marry before meeting at least a few times in person?

You need to be in a person's presence for a while in order to pick up all the verbal and nonverbal cues. The atmosphere created by physical and mental presence is as important as surface attraction, if not more so. For example, what sort of environment do the two of you create? How spontaneous are you? How strong is your need for conversation? What about your openness, supportiveness and companionship?

If you don't feel a connection in person, the relationship might not last. These things can only be determined by face-to-face contact.

who, despite being medically healthy, dies a few short months or even weeks after the death of the other spouse? Food and shelter aren't enough. We need each other, and we need love.

Why Likability Works

If people like you, they feel natural and comfortable around you. They will give you their attention and happily open up for you.

Likability has something to do with how you look but a lot more to do with how you make people feel. My old nanny, who brought me up to be passionate about people, used to talk about having "a sunny disposition." She'd take me out on the promenade, and we'd spot the people who had sunny dispositions and all those who were "sourpusses." She told me we can choose what we want to be, and then we'd laugh at the sourpusses because they looked so serious.

Likable people give loud and clear signals of their willingness to be sociable; they reveal that their public communication channels are open. Embedded in these signals is evidence of self-confidence, sincerity and trust. Likable people expose a warm, easygoing public face with an outgoing radiance that states, "I am ready to connect. I am open for business." They are welcoming and friendly, and they get other people's attention.

Why 90 Seconds?

"Time is precious." "Time costs money." "Don't waste my time." Time has become an increasingly sought-after commodity. We budget our time, make it stand still, slow it down or speed it up, lose sense of it and distort it; we even buy timesaving devices. Yet time is one of the few things we can't save—it is forever unfolding.

In bygone days, we were inherently more respectful of one another and devoted more time to the niceties of getting to know someone and explore common ground. In the hustle and bustle of life today, we rush about with so many deadlines attached to everything that unfortunately we don't have the time, or take the time, to invest in getting to know each other well. We look for associations, make appraisals and assumptions, and form decisions all within a few seconds and frequently before a word is even spoken. Friend or foe? Fight or flight? Opportunity or threat? Familiar or foreign?

Instinctively, we assess, undress and best-guess each other. And if we can't present ourselves fast and favorably, we run the risk of being politely, or impolitely, passed over.

The second reason for establishing likability in 90 seconds or less has to do with the human attention span. Believe it or not, the attention span of the average person is about 30 seconds! Focusing attention has been compared to controlling a troop of wild monkeys. Attention craves novelty—it needs to be entertained and loves to leap from branch to branch, making new connections. If there's nothing fresh and exciting for it to focus on, it becomes distracted and wanders off in search of something more compelling—deadlines, football or world peace.

Read this sentence, then look away from the book and fix your attention on anything that isn't moving (a great piece of art doesn't count). Keep your eyes on the object for 30 seconds. You'll probably feel your eyes glazing over after just 10 seconds, if not before.

In face-to-face communication, it's not enough to command the other person's attention. You must also be able to hold on to it long enough to deliver your message or intention. You will capture attention with your likability, but you will hold on to it with the quality of rapport you establish. More and more it comes down to three things: 1) your presence, i.e., what you look like and how you move; 2) your attitude, i.e., what you say, how you say it and how interesting you are; and 3) how you make people feel.

When you learn how to make fast, meaningful connections with people, you will improve your relationships at work and even at home. You will discover the enjoyment of being able to approach anyone with confidence and sincerity. But a word of caution: we're not about to change your personality; this is not a new way of being, not a new way of life. You are not getting a magic wand to rush out into the street with and have the world inviting you to dinner—these are connecting skills to be used only when you need them.

Establishing rapport in 90 seconds or less with another person or group, be it in a social or community setting or with a business audience or even in a packed courtroom, can be intimidating for many people. It has always amazed me that in this most fundamental of all life skills, we've been given little or no training. You are about to discover that you already possess many of the abilities needed for making natural connections with other people—it's just that you were never aware of them before.

First Impressions

For the purposes of this book, there are three parts to connecting with other people: meeting, establishing rapport and communicating. These three parts happen quickly and tend to overlap and blend into each other. Our goal is to make them as natural, fluid and easy as possible, and above all to make them enjoyable and rewarding.

Obviously, you begin the connecting process by meeting people. Sometimes you meet someone by chance—the woman on the train who turns out to share your passion for Bogart movies. And sometimes it's by choice—the man your cousin introduced you to because he loves Shakespeare, fine wines and bungee jumping, just like you.

If meeting is the physical coming together of two or more people, then communicating is what we do from the moment we are fully aware of another's presence. And between these two events—meeting and communicating—lies the 90-second land of rapport that links them together.

The Meeting

If you make the right impression during the first three or four seconds of a new meeting, you create an awareness that you are sincere, safe and trustworthy and the opportunity to go further and create rapport will present itself.

The Greeting

We call the first few seconds of contact the "greeting." Greetings are broken into five parts: Open—Eye—Beam—Hi!—Lean. These five actions constitute a welcoming program to carry out in a first encounter.

Open. The first part of the greeting is to open your attitude and your body. For this to work successfully, you must have already decided on a positive attitude that's right for you. This is the time to really feel and be aware of it.

Check to see that your body language is open. If you have the right attitude, this should take care of itself. Keep your heart aimed directly at the person you're meeting. Don't cover your heart with your hands or arms and, when possible, unbutton your jacket or coat.

Eye. The second part of the greeting involves your eyes. Be first with eye contact. Look this new person directly in the eye. Let your eyes reflect your positive attitude. To state the obvious: eye contact is *real* contact!

Get used to really looking at other people's eyes. When you're watching TV one evening, note the eye color of as many people as possible and say the name of the color to yourself. The next day, do the same with every person you meet, looking him or her straight in the eye.

Beam. This part is closely related to eye contact. Beam! Be the first to smile. Let your smile reflect your attitude.

Now you've gained the other person's attention through your open body language, your eye contact and your beaming smile. What that person is picking up subconsciously is an impression not of some grinning, gawking fool (though you may briefly fear you look like one!) but of someone who is completely sincere.

Hi! Whether it's "Hi!" or "Hello!" or even "Yo!" say it with pleasing tonality and attach your own name to it ("Hi! I'm Naomi"). As with the smile and the eye contact, be the first to identify yourself. It is at this point, and within only a few seconds, that you are in a position to gather tons of free information about the person you're meeting—information you can put to good use later in your conversation.

Take the lead. Extend your hand to the other person, and if it's convenient find a way to say his or her name two or three times to help fix it in memory. Not "Glenda,

Glenda, Glenda, nice to meet you" but "Glenda. Great to meet you, Glenda!" As you'll see in Chapter 7, this will be followed by your "occasion/location statement."

Lean. The final part of introducing yourself is the "lean." This action can be an almost imperceptible forward tilt to very subtly indicate your interest and openness as you begin to "synchronize" the person you've just met.

The Handshake

Handshakes run the gamut from the strong, sturdy bone-crusher to the wet noodle. Both are memorable—once shaken, twice shy, in some cases.

Certain expectations accompany a handshake. It should be firm and respectful, as if you were ringing a hand bell for room service. Deviate from these expectations and the other person will scramble to make sense of what's happening. There is a feeling that something is wrong—like hot water coming out of the cold tap. The brain hates confusion, and when faced with it the first instinct is to withdraw.

The "hands-free" handshake is a handshake without the hand, and it is a powerful tool. Just do everything you would do during a normal handshake but without using your hand. Point your heart at the other person and say hello. Light up your eyes and smile, and give off that same special energy that usually accompanies the full-blown shake.

Firing Energy

Nothing says more about your likeability and approachability in a flash than the quality and the level of energy you give off. You can try this in class or at work but two people can do it just as well.

With your group, make a circle about 12 feet across. Decide who is going to begin. That person chooses someone across from them in the circle, gathers up all the energy they can throughout their body and stores it in their heart. Then, all at once that person looks the other in the eye, says "Hi!", claps their hands together and points their right (the handshake hand) directly at the person's heart: firing all the energy stored inside them in a flash.

This is a long description of something that takes no more than a second, but when all six channels—body, heart, eyes, smile, clap and voice/breath—are fired in a rapid flash there is a vast transfer of energy.

Immediately after receiving the energy, the other person should fire it at someone else in the circle in the same way. Continue, fast and focused, firing energy at each other until everyone has been struck at least three times. Be sure to make contact with all six channels at once.

As a variation, you can choose to fire different qualities of energy: logic/head energy, ➡

communication/throat energy, love/heart energy, power/solar plexus energy and sexual energy. You've already fired love/heart energy.

Now, with a single partner do the same head to head instead of heart to heart. Keep firing logic/head energy at each other until you both agree that you can feel and differentiate it from love/heart energy. After two or three minutes sending energy back and forth, try the other regions: throat to throat, solar plexus to solar plexus, etc.

It gets even better. Figure out which kind of energy you want to send, but don't say what it is. Now greet your partner, shake hands, say "Hi" and fire! The goal is for your partner to identify the kind of energy he or she is receiving. Practice and practice until your body language becomes subtle and almost imperceptible.

Next, go out and try it on the people you meet. Fire energy when you say "Hi" to someone in a supermarket, to your waiter in the cafe, to your sister-in-law or the guy who fixes the photocopier in your office. They will notice something special about you—some might call it "star quality."

Incidentally, the "hands-free" handshake works wonders in presentations when you want to establish rapport with a group or audience.

Establishing Rapport

R apport is the establishment of common ground, of a comfort zone where two or more people can mentally join together. When you have rapport, each of you brings something *to* the interaction—attentiveness, warmth, a sense of humor, for example—and each brings something *back*: empathy, sympathy, maybe a couple of great jokes. Rapport is the lubricant that allows social exchanges to flow smoothly.

The prize, when you achieve rapport, is the other person's positive acceptance. This response won't be in so many words, but it will signal something like this: "I know I just met you, but I like you so I will trust you with my attention." Sometimes rapport just happens all by itself, as if by chance; sometimes you have to give it a hand. Get it right, and the communicating can begin. Get it wrong, and you'll have to bargain for attention.

As you meet and greet new people, your ability to establish rapport will depend on four things: your attitude, your ability to "synchronize" certain aspects of behavior like body language and voice tone, your conversation skills and your ability to discover which sense (Visual, Auditory or Kinesthetic) the other person relies on most. Once you become adept in these four areas, you will be able to quickly connect and establish rapport with anyone you choose and at any time.

Read on, and you'll discover that it's possible to speed up the process of feeling comfortable with a stranger by quantum-leaping the usual familiarization rituals and going straight into the routines that people who like each other do naturally. In virtually no time at all, you will be getting along as if you've known each other for ages. Many of my students report that when achieving rapport becomes second nature, they find people asking, "Are you sure we haven't met before?" I know the feeling; it happens to me all the time. And it's not just people asking me the question. I am convinced that half the people I meet, I've met before—that's the way it goes when you move easily into another person's map of the world. It's a wonderful feeling.

Communicating

Everyone seems to have a different sense of the word "communication," but the definitions usually go something like this: "It's an exchange of information between two or more people" . . . "It's getting your message across" . . . "It's being understood."

In the early days of Neuro-Linguistic Programming (NLP), a research project devoted to "the study of excellence and a model of how individuals structure their subjective sensory experience," Richard Bandler and John Grinder created an effective definition: "The meaning of communication lies in the response it gets." This is simple, and brilliant, because it means that it's 100% up to you whether or not your own communication succeeds. After all, *you* are the one with a message to deliver or a goal to achieve, and *you* are the one with the responsibility to make it happen. What's more, if it doesn't work, *you* are the one with the flexibility to change what you do until you finally get what you want. In order to give some form and function to communication here, let's assume that we have some kind of response or outcome in mind. People who are low on communication skills usually have not thought out the response they want from the other person in the first place and therefore cannot aim for it.

The skills you will learn here will serve you on all levels of communication, from social dealings like developing new relationships and being understood in your daily interactions all the way to life-changing moves for yourself and those in your sphere of influence.

The formula for effective communication has three distinct parts:

Know what you want. Formulate your intention in the affirmative and preferably in the present tense. For example, "I want a successful relationship, I have filled my imagination with what that relationship will look, sound, feel, smell and taste like with me in it, and I know when I will have it" is an affirmative statement, as opposed to "I don't want to be lonely."

Find out what you're getting. Assess what you're doing to acheive your goal and the response it's getting. For example, you may discover that going to bars isn't a great way for you to meet people.

Change what you do until you get what you want. Design a plan and follow through with it: "I'll invite three friends for dinner Saturday night and ask them each to bring someone." Do it and get more feedback. Redesign your plan if necessary, and do it again, evaluating whether it works better. Repeat the cycle—redesign–do–get feedback—until you get what you want. You can apply this cycle to any area of your life that you want to improve—finance, romance, sports, career, you name it.

- **K**now what you want.
- **F**ind out what you're getting.
- **C**hange what you do until you get what you want.

This is terrifically easy to remember because a certain Colonel had the good sense to open a chain of restaurants using the abbreviation KFC for a name. Every time we see one of his signs, we can use it as a reminder to ask ourselves how well the development of our communication skills is going.

What's Coming Up . . .

I n the following chapters, we'll examine the arena of rapport in much more detail, as well as the value of a Really Useful Attitude in projecting a positive image of yourself. You'll learn what happens at first sight on the surface and below the surface and the importance of having your body language, your voice tone and your words be congruent, or all saying the same thing. No crossed signals, no mixed messages, no confusion. You'll discover how your body language appeals to some but not others and how, by making a few adjustments to your own movements, you can positively affect the way people feel about you.

Then we'll delve deep into the warm and welcoming world of synchrony. You'll learn how to align yourself with the signals other people send you so that they'll feel a natural familiarity and comfort around you. We'll also discuss the massive importance of voice tone and how it influences the moods and emotions we want to convey.

A whole chapter is devoted to starting and maintaining sparkling conversation. We'll explore all the ways to open people up and avoid closing them down. We'll also deal with compliments, obtaining free information and being memorable.

Finally we'll go even deeper, down to the very core

of the human psyche. The astonishing truth is that although we navigate the world through our five senses, each of us has one sense that we rely on more than the other four. I'll show you how people are giving clues about their favorite sense all the time and how you can move onto the same sensory wavelength as theirs. Do people who rely mainly on their ears differ from those who rely mainly on their eyes? Darn right they do, and you'll find out how to tailor your approach to communicate with them.

Each chapter includes at least one exercise that will help you realize the power of connecting. Some of these exercises can be done alone, but others you have to do with a partner. Let's face it, face-to-face communication and rapport skills are interactive activities—you can't learn to do all of them all by yourself.

At the end of the book is a workbook with 21 more exercises designed to help you cement and put into practice what you've learned.

So there it is. Connecting. All day long, men, women and children give away vital keys to what makes them tick—to how they experience and filter the world—through their body language, their tone of voice, their eye movements and their choice of words. They simply cannot help doing this. Now it's up to you to learn how to use this wonderful, nonstop flood of information to achieve improved outcomes and more satisfying relationships.

The
90-Second
Land of
Rapport

Part Two

3

"There's Something About This Person I Really Like!"

Whether you're trying to make a sale, get a date or wangle out of a traffic ticket, you need to establish rapport. Sometimes rapport just happens naturally and you've no clue why. The job gets done, the conversation flows, the cop tears up the ticket. But how often have you found yourself in a situation where, no matter how hard you try, you just can't seem to connect with another person—and it makes no sense? After all, you know you're a fine, decent human being. Maybe you're even a fabulous, wildly attractive human being. But no matter what you say or do, you don't establish rapport and you can't connect.

You're not alone. Being a decent sort is not enough to guarantee good rapport with another person. In the dictionary, "rapport" is defined as "harmonious or sympathetic communication." In our interpersonal communications, we go through certain routines when we first meet a new person. If these routines work out and rapport is established, we can begin to deliver our communication with some certainty that it will be accepted and given serious consideration. Serious consideration is vital because the fundamental outcome of rapport is the perception of credibility, which in turn will lead to mutual trust. If credibility is not established, the messenger and not the message may become the focus of attention, and that attention will harbor discomfort.

But when we experience the world through the same eyes, ears and feelings as others, we are so bonded, or synchronized, with them that they can't help but know we understand them. This means being so much like them that they trust us and feel comfortable with us— that they say to themselves subconsciously, "I don't know what it is about this person, but there's something I really like."

Research has shown that we have approximately 90 seconds to make a favorable impression when we first meet someone. What happens in those 90 seconds can determine whether we succeed or fail at achieving rapport. In fact, frequently we have even less than 90 seconds!

Natural Rapport

Attraction is present everywhere in the universe. Whether you want to call it magnetism, polarity, electricity, thought, intelligence or charisma, it's still attraction, and it invests everything—animal, vegetable or mineral. We form synchronized partnerships naturally, and although they are hardly noticeable to some, they are quite tangible to others.

We have always relied on emotional contact and signals from our parents, peers, teachers and friends to guide us through our lives. We are influenced by their emotional feedback, their gestures and their way of doing things. When your mother or father sat a certain way, you would do the same; if a cool friend or a movie star walks a certain way, you might adopt a similar gait. We learn by aligning ourselves with the signals other people send us. They impress their way of being on us. We synchronize what we like about them.

People with common interests have natural rapport. The reason you get along so well with your close friends is that you have similar interests, similar opinions and maybe even similar ways of doing things. Sure, you will often find plenty to differ on and argue about, but essentially you are very much like each other.

We human beings are social animals. We live in

communities. It's far more "normal" and even logical for people to get along with one another than it is for them to argue, fight and *not* get along. The irony is that society has conditioned us to be afraid of each other—to set up boundaries between ourselves and others. We live in a society that pretends to find its unity through love but in actuality finds it through fear. The media scare us half to death with headlines and advertisements continually telling us of earthquakes and airplane crashes and asking us if we have enough insurance, are we too fat, too thin, does the smoke detector work and what about those high funeral expenses? Natural rapport is a prime requirement for our sanity, our evolution and, indeed, our survival.

Rapport by Chance

Perhaps you have traveled abroad to a country where people don't speak your language and you don't understand theirs. You feel a little uncomfortable—even suspicious—when you can't be understood. Then suddenly you meet someone from your own country, maybe your own state. This person speaks your language, and whammo, you have a new best friend—for your vacation at least. You might share experiences, opinions, insights, where to find the best restaurants and bargains. You will doubtless exchange personal information about family and work. All this and much more because you share a language. That's rapport by chance. Maybe your enthusiasm will lead you to continue that friendship after returning home, only to discover that apart from language and location the two of you have nothing in common and the relationship fizzles out all by itself.

This isn't limited to language and geography. Chance encounters happen on almost a daily basis to all of us—at work, in the supermarket, at the Laundromat or the bus stop.

The key to establishing rapport with strangers is to learn how to become like them. Fortunately, this is both very simple and a lot of fun to do. It allows you to look on each new encounter as a puzzle, a game, a joy.

Rapport by Design

When the interests or the behavior of two or more people are synchronized, these people are said to be in rapport. As we already know, rapport can happen in response to a shared interest or when you find yourself in certain situations or circumstances. But when none of these conditions is present, there is a way to establish rapport "by design"—and that's what this book is about.

Common Ground

Mark is attending a formal dinner, eight to a table. He hates coming to these events and as usual is stuck for words. He's beginning to get that squirmy feeling. He doesn't know anyone except for his accountant, who's sitting at the other end of the banquet hall and making everyone laugh. Suddenly the guest across from him, a young woman in a shiny blue dress who caught his eye a few moments ago even though they hadn't spoken, tells the man on her left that she is an avid stamp collector. Just like Mark!

Mark is relieved and overjoyed because chance has given him an excuse to talk to her. They have something in common—stamps. Mark speaks up and tells Tanya all about his rare 1948 *Poached Egg* stamp and how he found it when his Pontiac broke down in Cortlandville in upstate New York. With both elbows on the edge of the table and a finger poised gently ➡

When we set out to establish rapport by design, we purposely reduce the distance and differences between another person and ourselves by finding common ground. When this happens, we feel a natural connection with the person, or persons, because we are akin—we have become like each other.

As rapport develops between Mark and Tanya in the

on her cheek, close to her ear, Tanya leans toward Mark; her pupils dilate slightly as her shoulders become softer and more relaxed. Mark too leans forward on his elbows, smiling as Tanya smiles, nodding as she nods. She sips her water; he finds himself doing the same . . .

Mark and Tanya have established rapport. They connected and initiated a relationship through a common interest. Their rapport is evident on many levels—the cues and rhythms they are taking from and sending to each other, the imperceptible modifications of behavior they are making without thinking. The shared interest has given them proximity, and they are adjusting to one another. Who knows where it will lead? They like each other because they are like each other, and the dance of rapport has begun to calibrate itself. They have made a favorable connection in 90 seconds or less.

story box above, there is a lot more going on than meets the eye. The average person would perhaps not notice, but to the trained eye and ear there is plenty happening. As their shared interest in stamps emerges, so does a similarity in their behavior toward each other. Body language, facial expressions, tone of voice, eye contact, breathing patterns, body rhythms and many more physiological activities come into alignment. Simply put, they unconsciously start to behave in a like manner. They start synchronizing their actions.

Rapport by design is established by deliberately altering your behavior, just for a short time, in order to become *like* the other person. You become an adapter, just long enough to establish a connection. Precisely what you can adapt and how to do it is what you are about to learn in the chapters that follow.

All you will need at your disposal is your attitude, your appearance, your body, your facial expressions, your eyes, the tone and rhythms of your voice, your talent for structuring words into engaging conversation and your about-to-be-revealed gift for discovering another person's favorite sense. Add to this an ability to listen to and observe other people and a very large helping of curiosity. No gadgets, no appliances, no aphrodisiacs, no pills, no checkbook, no big stick. Just the wonderful gifts you were born with—and your heartwarming desire for the company of other people.

Attitude Is Everything

Y
our mind and your body are part of the same system. They influence each other. When you're happy, you look happy, you sound happy and you use happy words. Try to be miserable while you jump in the air and clap your hands, or try to be happy as you slouch in a chair and let your head droop. Your attitude controls your mind, and your mind delivers the body language.

Attitudes set the quality and mood of your thoughts, your voice tone, your spoken words. Most importantly, they govern your facial and body language. Attitudes are like trays on which we serve ourselves up to other people. Once your mind is set into a particular attitude, you have very little ongoing conscious control over the signals your body sends out. Your body has a mind of its own, and it will play out the patterns of behavior associated with whatever attitude you find yourself experiencing.

A Really *Useful* Attitude

No matter what you do or where you live, the quality of your attitude determines the quality of your relationships—not to mention just about everything else in your life.

I have been using the same bank branch for the last eight years. From time to time, someone I've never heard of before sends me a letter (spelling my name wrong) to tell me what a pleasure it is to have me as a special customer. No matter how hard they try to improve their "personalized" service, however, banks are pretty much the same all over, and my bank is really no different from the rest. So why do I still bank there even though two new, competing banks have recently opened much closer to where I live? Convenience? Obviously not. Better rates? Nope. More services? No. It's none of these things. It's Louanne, one of the tellers. What does Louanne offer that the institution can't? She makes me feel good. I believe she cares about me, and other customers feel the same way about her. You can tell by the way they talk with her. This charming lady brightens up the whole place.

How does Louanne do it? Simple. She knows what she wants: to please the customers and do her job well. She has a Really Useful Attitude or, to be more precise, two fully congruent Really Useful Attitudes. She is both cheery and interested, and everybody benefits: me the customer, her colleagues, her company, no doubt her family and, above all, herself. What Louanne sends out with her Really Useful Attitude comes back to her a thousandfold and becomes a joyous, self-fulfilling reality. And it doesn't cost a cent.

A Really *Useless* Attitude

Any two people can have wildly different attitudes toward the same set of experiences. However, when two people react to the same experience with the same attitude, they share a powerful natural bond. Attitudes have the tendency to be infectious, and because they are rooted in emotional interpretation of experiences, they can be distorted and shaped; they can be wound up or wound down.

What happens when people lose control and become angry? They look belligerent (body language), their voice tone is harsh and they use menacing words. They can be very scary to be around. From the point of view of making people like you, or even getting willing cooperation, we call this a Really Useless Attitude. How often have you seen infuriated parents berating their children for knocking over the bananas at the supermarket? Or bored, uninterested shop assistants? Or cranky, impatient doctors? They are all putting out useless attitudes.

I'm not saying whether this is right or wrong; I'm just pointing out that from a communications standpoint it doesn't deliver the message very well. Assuming they have a message. And that's often the point. Useless attitudes tend to come from people who don't know what they really want from their communication.

Remember, the "K" in "KFC" stands for "Know what you want." If you don't know what you want, there's no message to deliver and no basis for connecting with other people.

Most people think in terms of what they *don't* want as opposed to what they *do* want, and their attitudes reflect this. "I don't want my boss yelling at me anymore" comes with a whole different attitude than "I want my boss's job" or "I want to be promoted." Similarly, "I'm sick of selling neckties all day long" sends a completely different attitude and set of signals to your imagination than does "I want to run a charter fishing boat in Honey Harbor."

Your imagination is the strongest force that you possess—stronger than willpower. Think about it. Your imagination projects sensory experiences in your mind through the language of pictures, sounds, feelings, smells and tastes. Your imagination distorts reality. It can work for you or against you. It can make you feel terrific or miserable. So the better the information you can feed into your imagination, the better it can organize your thinking and your attitudes and ultimately your life.

It's Your Choice

The good news is that attitudes are yours to select. And if you're free to choose any one you please, why not choose a Really Useful Attitude?

Let's say you just flew into Miami International Airport and you missed your connection for Omaha. You simply have to get on the next flight at all costs, so you go up to the airline desk and shout at the representative. This is a Really Useless Attitude. If what you want is to get the attendant's maximum help, the best thing you can do is to find a Really Useful Attitude that will create rapport and get his cooperation.

I'll probably regret saying this, but I've talked my way out of dozens of automobile-related tickets (I've also failed a few times) and not just for parking infractions. I'm absolutely convinced that if I'd started by telling the officer his radar was off or by losing my temper and getting angry and telling him I'm the mayor's cousin and I'll never visit this town again, I'd be doomed from the start. If I want the officer to like me, to be understanding and not give me a ticket, then I have to assume a Really Useful Attitude like "I'm sorry" or "Fair enough" or "My, what a fool I am" or "Oh wow, yes, thanks!"

The last time I got stopped, the officer followed me into the village supermarket parking lot and pulled to a stop across the back of my car; I got out and walked to his car. From his physical appearance, with his beard and body set, I figured he was a Kinesthetic, or feeling-based person (you'll learn more about this later), so the first words out of my mouth were "Fair and square." That's because there was no doubt I was in the wrong. He gave me a well-deserved speech about what I'd done and let me off with a warning. The point is that my attitude set the tone of the encounter—because I knew what I wanted.

In face-to-face situations, your attitude precedes you. It is the central force in your life—it controls the quality and appearance of everything you do.

It doesn't take much imagination to dream up some Really Useless Attitudes—anger, impatience, conceit, boredom, cynicism—so why not take a moment to contemplate and feel a Really Useful Attitude? When you meet someone for the first time, you can be curious, enthusiastic, inquiring, helpful or engaging. Or my favorite—warm. There's something intoxicating about

Really Useful Attitudes	Really Useless Attitudes
Warm	Angry
Enthusiastic	Sarcastic
Confident	Impatient
Supportive	Bored
Relaxed	Disrespectful
Obliging	Conceited
Curious	Pessimistic
Resourceful	Anxious
Comfortable	Rude
Helpful	Suspicious
Engaging	Vengeful
Laid back	Afraid
Patient	Self-conscious
Welcoming	Mocking
Cheery	Embarrassed
Interested	Dutiful

warm human contact; in fact, scientists have discovered that it can generate the release of opiates in the brain—how about that for a Really Useful Attitude? Needless to say, any of these are more useful than revenge and disrespect.

Ask yourself, "What do I want, right now, at this moment? And which attitude will serve me best?" Remember, there are only two types of attitudes to consider

---

An Exercise in Attitude

Triggering Happy Memories

You know how certain sounds can remind you of something special in your life? When I was eight, my mother took me to a resort where I stood next to a man making fresh doughnuts while Paul Anka sang "Diana" in the background. Now, whenever I hear this song, it triggers the smell of fresh doughnuts and the memory of that happy holiday. It's the song that triggers the memory. A trigger can be a sound or something visual. It can also be a feeling or action. And believe it or not, it can be a clenched fist.

Follow the steps below, and you'll see what I mean. Use the hand you write with and clench your fist tightly. Then release. Repeat the action a couple of times. This will be your trigger.

1. *Pick a Really Useful Attitude*—one that you know will be useful when you first meet someone. It can be curious, resourceful, warm or patient, or any attitude you think will work for you. But it must be one that you have experienced at some time in your life and can recall on demand.

2. *Find a comfortable spot,* quiet and not too bright, where you won't be disturbed for 10 minutes. Sit down, place both feet on the floor, breathe slowly into your abdomen (not your chest) and relax. ➡

---

3. *Now you're ready.* Close your eyes and picture a time in your life when you felt the attitude you have chosen. In your mind's eye, make a picture of this specific event. Put in all the detail you can remember. What was in the foreground and background? Is the picture sharp or fuzzy, black-and-white or color? Is it large or small? Take your time and make it as real as you can. Now step into that picture and look out through your own eyes. Take note of what you see.

4. *Next, bring up the sounds associated with this picture.* Notice where the sounds come from: the left, the right, in front or behind? How loud or soft are they? What kinds of sounds are they? Music? Voices? Listen to the tone and the volume and the rhythm. Listen deeply, and the sounds will come flooding back. Listen to the quality of each sound and try to hear how it contributes to your chosen attitude.

5. *Bring in the physical sensations associated with the event:* the feel of the things around you, the air temperature, your clothing, your hair, what you're standing or sitting on. Next, notice the feelings inside your body. Where do they begin? Perhaps they move around in your body. Move your concentration deep into these wonderful feelings and enjoy them. Ride with them. Notice any smells and tastes that want to be included, and savor them, too. ➡

6. *With your "outside" eyes still closed,* look out through your "inside" eyes again at the scene. Make the pictures sharper, brighter, bolder and bigger. Make the sounds stronger, clearer, purer and more perfect. Make the feelings stronger, richer, deeper, warmer. Follow the intensity of the feelings if they move from one place to another, then loop them back to the beginning and intensify them. Loop them over and over as they get stronger and stronger. Let the feeling flood all over you.

7. *Make everything twice as big and strong and pure.* Then double it again. And again. Now your whole body and mind are luxuriating in the experience of it all. Seeing it, hearing it, feeling it. Make the sensations as strong as you can, and just when you can't make them any stronger, double them one more time and clench your fist hard and fast as you anchor the height of the experience to your trigger. Feel the sensations pour through you. Intensify them again, then clench your fist at the height of the feelings and release. Relax your hand and feel the sensations pour through your body. Do this one more time, then relax your hand and the rest of your body. Come down in your own time and relax.

Wait a minute or so, then test your trigger. Make a tight fist and notice the feelings rush into all your senses. Test it again after a couple of minutes. You are ready to use this Really Useful Attitude whenever you want.

when we are dealing with fellow humans: useful and useless.

How many times have you seen a newsmaker give a TV interview when she's frustrated? Or a salesperson serve you in a store when he clearly wishes he were somewhere else, a colleague who is sarcastic to the very person who can get the photocopying done faster if desired, or passengers being rude to the cab driver who is the only person with the means to get them to the church on time? These are all Really Useless Attitudes. As far as communication is concerned, they are virtually guaranteed to fail.

A Really Useful Attitude is one of the major delivery vehicles of the likability factor—and it works like a charm. Your posture, your movements and your expression will speak volumes about you before you even open your mouth.

The sooner you know what you want and which is the most useful attitude to help you get it, the sooner your body language and your voice and your words will change to help you get it.

The conclusion is obvious. People who know what they want tend to get it because they are focused and positive, and this is reflected outward and inward in their attitude. Take on a cheery attitude the next time you meet someone new and see how your whole being changes to the part. Your look will be cheery, you'll sound cheery and you'll use cheery words. This is the full "communication package." Other people make major adjustments in their responses to you based on the signals you transmit. The next chapter will take a detailed look at how these signals combine to present a positive image.

5

Actions *Do* Speak Louder Than Words

First impressions are powerful. Along with the instinctive fight-or-flight appraisals, we are also weighing the opportunities involved in almost every new face-to-face encounter.

No matter how hard we try, we cannot get away from the fact that image and appearance are important when meeting someone for the first time. Dressing well goes a long way toward making a positive impression as you begin to establish rapport, but how do you make people warm to you? And how do you project the likable parts of your own unique personality?

Body Language

Your body language, which includes your posture, your expressions and your gestures, accounts for more than half of what other people respond to and make assumptions about.

When we think of body language, we tend to think it means what happens from the neck down. But much of what we communicate to others—and what they make assumptions about—comes from the neck up. Facial gestures and nods and tilts of the head have a vocabulary that equals or exceeds that of the rest of the body.

The signals we send with our bodies are rich with meaning and global in their scope. Some of them are hardwired into us at birth; others are picked up from our society and culture. Everywhere on the planet, panic induces an uncontrollable shielding of the heart with the hands and/or a freezing of the limbs. A smile is a smile on all continents, while sadness is displayed through down-turned lips as often in New York as in Papua New Guinea. The clenched fists of determination and the open palms of truth convey the same message in Iceland as they do in Indonesia.

And no matter where on earth you find yourself, mothers and fathers instinctively cradle their babies with the head against the left side of their body, close to the heart. The heart is at the heart of it all. Facial expressions and body language are all obedient to the greater purpose of helping your body maintain the well-being of its center of feeling, mood and emotion—your heart.

Volumes have been written about body language, but when all is said and done, this form of communication can be broken down into two rather broad categories: open and closed. Open body language exposes the heart, while closed body language defends or protects it. In establishing rapport, we can also think in terms of inclusive gestures and noninclusive gestures.

Open Body Language

Open body language exposes your heart and body (within limits of decency, of course!) and signals cooperation, agreement, willingness, enthusiasm and approval. These gestures are meant to be seen. They show trust. They say "YES!"

Your body doesn't know how to lie. Unconsciously, with no directions from you, it transmits your thoughts and feelings in a language of its own to the bodies of other people, and these bodies understand the language perfectly. Any contradictions in the language can interrupt the development of rapport.

In his classic work *How to Read a Person like a Book,* Gerard I. Nierenberg explains the value of open gestures. These gestures include open hands and uncrossed arms as well as the occasional subtle movement toward the other person that says "I am with you" and shows acceptance: an open coat or jacket, for example, both literally and symbolically exposes the heart. When used together, such gestures say "Things are going well."

Positive, open-body gestures reach out to others. These gestures are generally slow and deliberate. When an open person makes contact with the heart of another person, a strong connection is made and trust becomes possible. (You know the feeling of a good hug? Or a heart-to-heart talk? You can accomplish much the same feeling using open body language.)

When you meet someone new, immediately point your heart warmly at that person's heart. There is magic in this.

Other common open gestures include standing with your hands on your hips and your feet apart, a stance that shows enthusiasm and willingness, and moving forward in your chair (if accompanied by other open gestures). Leaning forward shows interest, and uncrossing your arms or legs signals you are open to suggestions.

Closed Body Language

Defensiveness is shown through gestures that protect the body and defend the heart. These gestures suggest resistance, frustration, anxiety, stubbornness, nervousness and impatience. They are negative gestures, and they say "NO!"

Crossed arms are common to all manifestations of defensiveness. They hide the heart and defend one's feelings. Although you can also be relatively relaxed with your arms crossed, the difference between a relaxed crossed-arm position and a defensive crossed-arm position is in the accompanying gestures. For example, are your arms loosely folded or pressed close to your body? Are your hands clenched or open?

Defensive gestures are often fast and evasive and beyond your conscious control. Your body has a mind of its own and is ruled by your attitude, useful or useless. In addition to crossed arms, the most obvious defensive gestures are avoiding eye contact with the other person and turning your body sideways. Fidgeting is another negative gesture, which can also show impatience or nervousness.

Right away, you can see the difference between a person who faces you squarely and honestly, and someone who stands sideways to you with crossed arms and hunched shoulders while the two of you talk. In the first instance, the person is openly pointing his heart directly at your heart. In the second, the posture is defensive; the person is pointing his heart away from you and protecting it. One is being open with you, the other closed. Being in the presence of these two postures produces very different feelings.

Smaller Gestures

Hand gestures are also part of the vocabulary of body language. They, too, can be divided into open gestures (positive responses) and closed or concealed gestures (negative responses), except that their range is far more intricate and expressive. I should point out that individual gestures, just like the individual words on this page, don't say much. Only when you're presented with more than one gesture, perhaps combined with an expression and topped off with some overall body language, can you deduce that a particular clenched fist means "Wow, my team won the playoffs!" and not "I'm so mad I want to slap him!"

A similar set of differences occurs in body language above the neck. The open face smiles, makes eye contact, gives feedback, shows curiosity and raises the eyebrows to show interest. In a casual encounter, a quick look and a lowering of the eyes says "I trust you. I'm not afraid of you." A prolonged look strengthens the positive signal. In conversation, we may use a nod of the head at the end of a statement to indicate that an answer is expected.

In contrast, the closed face frowns, purses the lips and avoids eye contact. And there is yet another negative category to add to facial responses. We politely call it the neutral, or expressionless, face. It's the one that just gawks at you like a dead trout. In the next chapter, you'll find out how to react to this "non-face," which can be very disconcerting if you don't know how to deal with it.

Frequently I look around at my audiences and recognize people who have heard me talk before. I recognize them because they have "the look of recognition" on their face when they see me. It's a look, or even an attitude, of silent anticipation that any minute I'll recognize them. Well, this look can work wonders—from time to time—with people you haven't met before. If you're on your own, try it out right now. Let your mouth open slightly in a smile as your eyebrows arch and your head tilts back a little with anticipation as you look directly at an imaginary person. A variation is to tilt your head as you look slightly away and then look back at the person with the bare minimum of a frown and/or pursed lips. Practice. Then give it a try. Be as subtle as you possibly can.

Last spring, I rented a bus for my daughter and her friends to be chauffeured around in on the night of their prom. While I was paying at the rental office, I noticed a woman sitting at the next desk over. She had a look on her face that said she knew me, and I racked my brain to place her. I couldn't.

In the end I had to say, "I'm sorry, but have we met before?"

"No," she replied seriously. Then she stood up at her

Flirting

Classic flirting behavior involves letting someone know you like him or her and that you'd like to pursue it further. Not surprisingly, body language plays a huge part in this game, and even less surprisingly, so does eye contact. Dozens of little gestures are used to send out sexual messages: the tilt of the head, holding eye contact a little longer than normal, the angle of the hips and the hands through the hair. Glancing sideways is a gesture that can suggest doubt on its own, but combined with a slight smile and a narrowing of the eyes it is a powerful gesture of flirtation.

A man sends out signals with his swagger; a woman, by rolling her hips. A man loosens his tie ever so slightly; a woman moistens her lips. On and on, the parties convey their interest in each other through their stances, glances and postures until some small gesture synchronizes and sends the O.K.

desk, held out her hand to me and smiled. "Hi, I'm Natalie," she said.

I had been obliged to speak first, and she had done the polite thing. She had stood up, offered her hand, smiled and introduced herself. All completely innocent—or was it? I have no idea. But we had rapport, and she had me talking.

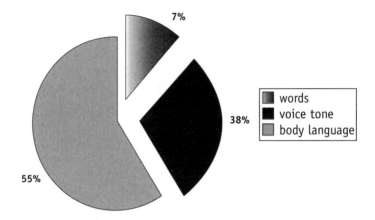

Congruity

Why do we like great actors and take them seriously when we know they're only speaking lines that someone else wrote? Because they are believable; because they are congruent.

In 1967, Albert Mehrabian, professor emeritus of psychology at UCLA, carried out the most widely quoted study on communication. He determined that believability depends on the consistency, or congruity, of three aspects of communication. In a paper titled "Decoding of Inconsistent Communication," he reported the percentages of a message expressed through our different communication channels in this way: interestingly, 55% of what we respond to takes place visually; 38% of what we respond to is the sound of

Mixed Messages

 Rosa, a waitress, folds up the ad she's torn from a newspaper, clears off the table where her new computer will sit and leaves her apartment.

At the electronics store, as Rosa hovers over the latest desktop model from Megahype, a young salesman notices the ad in her hand and wanders over to her. He unbuttons his jacket, spreads his hands out, palms up, and looks her in the eye. "I see you found it already," he says with a smile. "Hi, my name's Tony."

For the next 10 minutes, a relaxed and sincere Tony talks to Rosa. He faces her with his hands exposed and leans forward from time to time as they discuss the features of the computer. Rosa listens with interest, her head tilted to one side and her hand on her cheek, as Tony offers to "throw in" $95 of extras and even agrees to "eat the tax."

Finally, stroking her chin as she forms a decision, Rosa nods. "Yes," she says, "this is the model for me."

"Great," says Tony, eagerly rubbing his palms together. "It will take about five minutes to take it down and find some boxes."

Rosa looks sideways at him and frowns. "You don't have a new one in a box?"

"That might be hard to find right now." Tony's hands become fists, and he pops them into his ➡

pockets. "They're such an unbelievable deal—they've just been flying out of the store." He buttons up his jacket, shrugs his shoulders and laughs nervously.

"So this is a demonstration model?" Rosa tilts her head, inquiring.

"Just came on the floor this morning," Tony shoots back with an insincere smile. He folds his arms in front of his chest and turns himself sideways to her, pretending to be distracted by something going on in the TV department nearby. His voice falters and weakens as he says, "It has the same warranty as a new one."

Rosa rubs the side of her nose in doubt. "Came on the floor this morning? Fine. Can I have that in writing?"

Tony's back is turned to her as he leans over the monitor, fiddling with the cables—any excuse not to look at her. He catches a glimpse of himself in one of the wall mirrors. *Oh boy, what an idiot I am,* he thinks. He bites his lip and turns back to face Rosa.

But Rosa is gone.

As a good waitress, Rosa is used to reading body language. She saw that the salesman's gestures conflicted (lacked congruity) with his words, and she knew that she should believe the gestures. The change in Tony's voice tone from informing to pleading just served to confirm her feelings of doubt.

communication; and 7% of what we respond to involves the actual words we use.

The professor called these the three "V's" of communication: the visual, the vocal and the verbal. And to be believable, they must all give out the same message. This is at the very foundation of rapport by design. Over half of all communication is nonverbal! It is the look of the communication, our body language, that counts the most: the way we act, dress, move, gesture and so on.

Need proof? Think of the last time you were with someone who stood with her arms crossed, tapping her foot and looking annoyed, and then huffed the words "I'm fine." Which clues did you believe—the words or the body language and tone of voice? Physical messages often send a much louder message than spoken words. Because 55% of your communication occurs as body language, see how easy it is, whether consciously or not, to signal either openness or defensiveness to another person by means of your body language. Gestures, rather than words, are the true indicators of your instinctive reactions.

If you want others to believe that you can be trusted, you must be congruent. Your spoken language and your body language must say the same thing. If they don't, the other person's body will signal its discomfort to your body. In response to this communication, your

An Exercise in Congruity

Words vs. Tone

Say each phrase below with different tonality: anger, boredom, surprise and flirtatiousness. Notice how your body language, facial expression and breathing combine to alter your emotional state.

"It's late."

"I've had enough."

"Look at me."

"Where were you born?"

To check your tonality, find a friend and say one or two of these phrases. See if your friend can tell you which of the four feelings you're expressing. If it's not obvious, keep working at it until it's clear.

body will signal to your brain by mixing up a chemical cocktail that corresponds to the discomfort that the other person is feeling. Then you will *both* be uncomfortable, and rapport will be that much harder to achieve. When they notice a discrepancy between your words and gestures, other people will believe the gestures and react accordingly.

So, congruity occurs when your body, voice tone and words are all in alignment. And when your body, tone and words are communicating the same thing, you will appear sincere and people will tend to believe you. This is why a Really Useful Attitude is so important. Appearing sincere, or congruent, is a key ingredient for building the trust that opens the door to likability and rapport.

Make sure that your words, your tonality and your gestures are all saying the same thing. Be on the lookout for incongruity in others. Notice how it makes you feel.

We've all seen those old movies where a couple of people are driving along in a car, and they're rocking the steering wheel even though the background shows a road that's straight as an arrow. It's phony—you know they're really in a studio being bounced around in a box. Your senses have told you that something isn't right, something is out of alignment, and so you can't believe what you see. Or have you ever had someone get mad at you and then, in the middle of bawling you out, flash a sinister little smile that disappears as fast as it came? Very chilling. This is another example of incongruent behavior. The smile doesn't belong with the anger; it's insincere.

Recognizing incongruent behavior is another survival instinct. If you're on vacation and you're approached by a complete stranger who grins at you while he rubs his hands briskly together, licks his lips and says, "Good morning, how would you like to invest in the world's best time-share deal," the chances are you'll be on your guard. A quick congruence check is instinctive and is another reason why first impressions are paramount.

Frequently a person's emotions and intentions are misunderstood by those around them. For instance, a woman at one of my seminars discovered that she unconsciously used a tone of voice that was incongruent with her words. "No, I'm not confused, I'm interested," she would insist when tested. And again, "No, I'm not sad, I'm relaxed." This went on and on until she came to the verge of tears and said, "Now I know why my kids are always saying, 'Mom, how come you get mad at us all the time?' And I'm *not* mad at them. Sometimes I'm just excited."

The same woman also told us that her coworkers accused her of sarcasm but that, to her, nothing could be further from the truth. In fact, sarcasm is simply words said with conflicting voice tone. It is structured so the person on the receiving end will believe what's inferred by the tonality. Suppose you let your team down and somebody is heard to quip, "That was brilliant," with a tonality that communicates annoyance. It's a very different case when you score a fantastic goal and the same person is heard saying with excitement, "That was brilliant!"

Congruity, then, has one unshakable rule and it is this: if your gestures, tone and words do not say the same thing, people will believe the gestures. Go up to someone you know, purse your lips and say, "I really like you," with your eyebrows raised and your arms folded. Ask them what they think. Even better, go find a mirror and try it. Well? You get my point. Your gestures are a giveaway to what you really mean.

Being Yourself

Do you feel nervous when you meet someone new? Physiologically, being nervous and being excited have a lot in common: pounding heart, churning tummy, high chest breathing and the general jitters. But one of these states might send you hightailing it for the nearest dark corner while the other one can serve you well and propel you forward. There is a tendency for panic to accompany nervousness, and this quite naturally makes bodily activities speed up. Because much of your nervousness stems from increased awareness, try redirecting some of your awareness toward slowing down and being more deliberate. One great technique is to imagine that your nostrils are just below your navel and that your in-and-out breaths are happening down there. The slower you are, within reason, the more in control you will appear.

The sooner you start telling yourself that you're excited rather than nervous, the sooner you'll be able to convince your subconscious that this is actually how you feel. And, in fact, that's really all that matters. Change your attitude, and your body language and voice tone will change to reflect your new attitude. Keep in mind that most people are as eager as you are to establish rapport. They will generously give you the benefit of the doubt.

Don't try too hard! In a study conducted at Princeton University, students of both sexes were questioned about their methods of sizing up people they met for the first time. Overeagerness was one of the most reported turnoffs. Don't smile too hard, don't try to be too witty, don't be overpolite and avoid the temptation to be patronizing.

As you become more at ease with your attitude, people will begin to notice characteristics that are unique to you—that set you apart from the others and define you as an individual. You will naturally and easily project the likable parts of your own unique personality and have more conscious control and confidence in your ability to create rapport at will.

All relationships are built on trust. Trust is built on congruence. It doesn't matter whether you're selling real estate, designing concept cars, recommending the lamb chops over the chili, looking for the perfect partner or giving the State of the Union address, you have to fully connect with people. Fully connecting means that unconsciously, people will say to themselves, "I trust you, you make sense and you move me." Of these three, trust always comes first. Without congruence, you can never make someone like and trust you in 90 seconds or less.

6

People Like People Like Themselves

My neighbor down the road loves to fish. So do his two sons, who, by the way, look like their dad and walk like him. What a bond! I don't fish, and neither do any of my five children, but we share the same sense of humor. What a relief! My aunt in Scotland is a medical doctor, and so is her daughter. They think alike. Another coincidence? The plumber in our village comes from three generations of plumbers. The woman who sold me a big ripe Gouda cheese at the Wednesday market in Leiden, just outside Amsterdam, had her mother and her daughter working for her. All dressed the same.

What's going on here? Is there some kind of pattern emerging? How come they are so much alike? They have all grown up with harmonious behavior on many levels, physical and mental. They have synchrony.

Since he was only three years old, my neighbor's youngest son has handled a fishing rod with great respect, just like his dad. He sits a certain way, just like his dad, and when he's threading the hook, he glances at his father from moment to moment to see if he's doing it correctly: a certain, almost imperceptible expression says "continue," another says "be careful" and yet another says "no, you've got it wrong." The boy uses his own instincts to learn from his father, along with very subtle guidance from his father's expressions and body language and at times his gentle, encouraging voice. Now he can do it, just like his dad.

Natural Synchrony

We learn our life skills through guidance and rapport with others. As we continually pick up signals from our parents, peers, teachers, coaches, TV, movies and our environment, our behavior is modulated and organized by synchronizing ourselves with the conduct of others and adjusting to their emotional feedback. Unwittingly, we have been synchronizing ourselves with other people since birth. A baby's body rhythms are synchronized with those of her mother. An infant's mood is influenced by his father's mood, a child's favorite toys are selected to keep pace with her peers, a teen's tastes must conform to what's cool and an adult's preferences are influenced by partner, friends and the community.

All day long, we synchronize ourselves with those

around us. We do it all the time. We thrive on it, and we can't exist without it. We are always influencing each other's behavior; every moment we are with other people, we make minute adjustments to our behavior, and they to ours. This is what synchrony is all about. We process the signals unconsciously and transmit them to each other through our emotions. It is how we draw our strength and convictions; it is how we feel safe. It is how we evolve. And it is why people like, trust and feel comfortable with people who are just like them.

People hire people like themselves.
People buy from people like themselves.
People date people like themselves.
People lend money to people like themselves.
And so on—ad infinitum.

Perhaps you've noticed that you take to some people immediately upon meeting them for the first time and yet feel no rapport at all with other new people. Or you might even feel an instant dislike for some people. This is something we've all experienced, but have you ever stopped to wonder why this happens? Why is it that with certain people you feel the natural trust and comfort that comes with rapport? Think back over the last week to some of the people you met in your adventures. Go over the meetings in your mind and relive them.

What was it about the people you liked that made you like them? Chances are you shared something—interests or attitudes or ways of moving. People who get on well together usually have things in common. Those who share similar ideas, have the same taste in music or food, read similar books or like the same holidays, hobbies, sports or vacation spots will feel immediately comfortable with one another and like each other better than those who have nothing in common.

When I lecture, I go over to a large blackboard and write:

I LIKE YOU!

Then I add the tiny, two-letter word "am" between the first and second words of that joyous phrase so that it now reads:

I *AM* LIKE YOU!

The fact is that we like people who are like us. We are at ease with people who feel familiar (where do you think the word "familiar" comes from?). Look to your close friends. The reason you get along so well with them is that you have similar opinions, maybe even similar ways of doing things. Sure, you will often find plenty to differ on and argue about, but essentially you are like each other.

People with similar interests have natural rapport. If you share an interest in motor sports with one of the guys at the office, this can become a basis for rapport.

Or perhaps you have two toddlers and go to the park every afternoon to meet up with other mothers in the same circumstances; this is again a basis for rapport. You've heard the saying "Birds of a feather flock together"—well, quite simply, people are comfortable when they are surrounded by people like themselves.

Rapport by chance holds true not just on the surface but underneath as well. Shared beliefs, appearance, tastes and circumstance all contribute to rapport. Perhaps you feel comfortable around people with fluent, expressive voices or sensitive people who speak softly and slowly. Maybe you enjoy the company of people who share their feelings when they communicate or those who get straight to the point and don't mince their words. When you establish rapport by chance, you have come across someone who grew up with or developed a style similar to your own.

The Art of Synchronizing

But why wait for rapport to happen naturally? Why not go straight into synchronizing with other people's behavior as soon as you meet them? Why not invest 90 seconds or less of your time to establish rapport by design?

Look around any restaurant, coffee shop, mall or other public place where people meet each other and look around to see which ones are "in rapport" and which ones aren't. The ones who have rapport sit together in the same way. Notice how they lean toward one another. Notice their leg and arm positions. Those in rapport are synchronized almost like dancers: one picks up a cup, the other follows; one leans back, the other does the same; one talks softly, the other talks softly. The dance goes on: body position, rhythm, tone of voice. Now look for those people who are clearly together but not synchronized, and observe the differences. Which pairs or groups appear to be having a better time?

I recently gave a speech at an auditorium in London, and right there, about 10 rows back, was a beautiful couple. Both were immaculately dressed, with great attention to color and detail. When I noticed them, they were sitting in the identical position, leaning to the right with their hands folded close to their respective armrests. Then, as if responding to a prearranged signal, they both transferred their weight onto the other armrest, like synchronized swimmers, nodding and smiling in unison. They confirmed everything I was saying. I caught up with them afterward and learned that they had been married for 47 years; they were fit, healthy, happy and totally synchronized.

Our goal, then, is to discover the structure of synchrony and modify it to apply to the different types of people we meet. The key to establishing rapport is learning how to synchronize what Professor Mehrabian called the three "V's" of consistent human communication—the visual, the vocal and the verbal—in order to connect with other people by becoming as much like them as possible.

But doesn't this mean I'm being phony or insincere? No. You are doing what comes naturally. Watch a tree fall on someone in the movies and you flinch. See a wrestler get booted in the stomach and you wince. Someone smiles at you, you feel the urge to smile back; someone yawns, you want to yawn too; same goes for crying. We synchronize unconsciously all day long.

Synchronizing is a way of adapting to others. And remember, we're only talking about a minute and a half! You're not being asked to engineer a total personality change. All you are doing is speeding up what would happen naturally if you had more time. The idea is not to make your movements, tone and words obvious copies of the other person's, but rather to do the same kind of thing you do with a friend.

Often, when you travel in a foreign country, the plug of your hair dryer or electric shaver will just not fit into the outlet—you need an adapter to make it work, a connecting device that will let you plug the thing in and power it up. It's precisely the same thing when you plug into other people. Like the hair dryer or the electric shaver, you must have an adapter. So think of synchronizing as an adapting device that allows you to make smooth connections at will and quickly. Synchronizing is a way to make the other person become open, relaxed and happy to be with you. You just do what they do; you become like them until the other person thinks, *I don't know what it is about this person, but there's something I really like!*

Think of synchronizing as rowing your boat alongside another person's rowboat, pointing it in the same direction at the same speed and picking up the other person's pace, stroke, breathing pattern, mood and point of view. As he rows, you row.

One evening a few years ago, I was sitting in the chalet of a ski club, waiting for my two youngest children to finish night skiing. Suddenly in walked a neighbor, a lawyer who had been on polite "nodding" terms with my family. When I saw him arrive, I made up my mind to try out some simple synchronizing on him. I decided on the outcome I wanted (remember, know what you want) and that I would continue synchronizing until he made a definite gesture of friendship. I calmly stood up and he spotted me. We met in the middle of the large room.

"Hi there," he said with a tight-lipped smile as he shook my hand.

Matching the tone of his voice overall and his body stance, I echoed: "Hi there!"

He placed one hand on his hip, and with the other pointed out the chalet window. "Just waiting for my kids to finish!"

"Me, too," I said, mirroring his gestures. "I'm waiting for my kids to finish."

I synchronized him, respectfully, for less than 30 seconds of normal, innocent conversation. Then he suddenly blurted out, "You know something? We really don't see enough of you and your family. Why don't you come by for dinner one night?"

We set the date right there and then. I could almost read what had happened by the way his mouth twisted. He was thinking, *There's something about this guy I really like, but I'm not quite sure what it is.* Obviously, if he felt I'd been copying him, he'd have never issued the invitation!

I had approached him with a Really Useful Attitude of warmth that, even though I was synchronizing him, I kept fairly close to the surface. I faced him and immediately took on his overall posture and used similar gestures and facial expressions. The vocal part, his voice tone and speed, was easy to fall in with. And I used similar words. It sounds more complicated than it actually was. The whole thing took only a few seconds. It was fun and it felt good. I really did want to get to know him better, and this seemed the perfect opportunity. I'm sure we both experienced the thrill

The Bully

Mr. Szabo, the owner of a large chain of super-markets, is well known among the trade for his intimidating manner. One day, he summoned the product managers of three competitive, nationally rec-ognized brands to meet him at one of his outlets. He led the three product managers to the aisle in which their products were displayed and proceeded to scold them for what he perceived to be the disgraceful state of their product facing. As he waved his arms about, pointing out what was wrong, he raised and lowered his voice, occa-sionally pausing to stare at them individually and even jabbing one of them, Paul, on the shoulder with his fin-ger. At the end of his tirade, two of the browbeaten indi-viduals nodded and made excuses, which gave Mr. Szabo even more ammunition to use against them. ➡

that only people can generate in people—the thrill of making new connections. There is absolutely nothing in this world as exciting and rewarding as connecting and developing a rapport that can lead to a new friend-ship or relationship.

What about difficult people? I am often asked what you're supposed to do when you meet somebody who is all bundled up with defensiveness: tight jaw, arms crossed defensively or hands jammed into pockets. Or

Ever since Mr. Szabo had begun his rant, Paul had been skillfully synchronizing Szabo's mood and general mannerisms. When it came time for him to respond to the irate owner, he almost *became* Mr. Szabo—but in a completely nonthreatening way. He used similar arm gestures, tonality, pauses and attitude, and he even jabbed Mr. Szabo on the shoulder as he said, "You're absolutely right."

As they talked back and forth for a minute or so, Paul calmed down his own gestures, and Mr. Szabo followed. When they finished talking, Mr. Szabo put his arm around Paul's shoulder and led him to the end of the aisle. There he collared one of the store staff and said to him, "Give this man any help he needs."

Paul had successfully joined Mr. Szabo in his world and led him quickly, skillfully and respectfully to his own desired outcome.

the best way to handle a bully, a shy person, a complainer or someone who is arrogant or overly aggressive. It is not the purpose of this book to give detailed instructions on dealing with difficult people, but here are some guidelines.

Rule number one when encountering a difficult person is to ask yourself this question: "Do I really need to deal with this person?" If the answer is no, then leave him or her alone. If the answer is yes, ask yourself what it is that you want. What is your desired outcome? Not what you *don't* want. (Remember KFC? If not, see page 22.)

When synchronizing "difficult people," it's vital that you do it in a nonthreatening way. Once you have matched your body and tone with theirs, you can begin to "lead" them out of it. Unfold your arms, relax your shoulders and check to see if they follow your lead; if they don't, get back into your original position for a minute or so and try again.

A word about shy people: try to find out what they're interested in. Synchronize their body movements and voice tone, and unhurriedly ask them lots of open-ended questions (see the next chapter) until you get a glimmer of enthusiasm. Take on their attitude, and then little by little lead them out of it. Lean or sit forward and see if they follow; if not, go back to where you were and synchronize any little thing you can. You'll be surprised at how well this works.

When do I start synchronizing? Try not to let more than two or three seconds go by before you start. Remember the sequence in Chapter 2: Open (Really Useful Attitude and open body language)—Heart (pointed at the person)—Eye (first with the eye contact)—Beam (first with the smile)—"Hi!" (introduce yourself)—Lean (indicate interest as you start synchronizing).

Anything that increases the common ground and reduces the distance between you and the other person is a good thing. And the quickest way to accomplish this is to synchronize with the person—in other words, adopt the same attitude, overall body language and voice tone.

Synchronizing Attitude

Synchronizing attitude—or multiple congruity, to give it its scientific name—takes into account location and mood. It is also frequently supportive, as when a friend is challenged and you "take a stand" with him, or a parent deeply relates to a child's problem with a class assignment, or you share the exhilaration your partner feels over a promotion. When people "go through things together," they will often be synchronized right down to primal sighs of despair or shouts of joy.

Pick up on other people's feelings. Synchronize their movements, breathing pattern and expression as you "deeply identify" with them. Tune in to the overall mood suggested by their voice and reflect it back.

Synchronizing Body Language

As you already know, body language accounts for 55% of our communication. It is the most obvious, easiest and most rewarding feature to synchronize on your way to rapport. If you get nothing else out of this book but the ability to synchronize other people's body language, you'll be miles ahead of where you were last month.

Doing What Comes Naturally

Dave was out looking for an anniversary present for his wife. He had whittled his thinking down to two ideas. It was to be either the very latest cell phone or a painting to hang in their breakfast room.

From where Dave parked his car at the shopping mall, it was more convenient to visit the electronics store first. Fortunately, it was midmorning and the store wasn't too busy. Dave approached the counter, where a salesman in a flashy vest was nodding and smiling. So far, so good. As the salesman started to explain the differences in all the latest models, he lifted his right leg and plunked it on a low stool that was somewhere next to him. Then he leaned thoughtfully on his right knee and continued with his explanations. Suddenly Dave couldn't wait to get out of there. It wasn't that he lacked interest, it was just that the macho, leg-raised position was completely out of sync with his own posture and it made him feel uncomfortable.

Synchronizing body language falls into two loose groupings: *matching,* which means doing the same thing as the other person (she moves her left hand, you move your left hand), and *mirroring,* which means, as it implies, moving as if you were watching the other person in a mirror (he moves his left hand, you move your right).

It was a completely different story at the art gallery. Dave stopped before a painting that took his fancy and adopted a contemplative stance: weight on one leg, arms folded but with one hand on his chin and a finger hooked around his lips. After maybe a minute, he became aware of somebody standing quietly next to him and heard a soft, supportive voice say simply, "Nice, isn't it?"

"Yes, it is," Dave replied in a pensive voice.

"Let me know if I can help you," said the lady at his side. She withdrew to another part of the gallery.

Within five minutes, Dave had bought the painting. It seemed the natural thing to do.

Dave felt comfortable just looking at the painting. The woman had slipped in beside him, taken on the same body language as his and dropped into the same attitude. She made a seamless connection by exercising perfect, effortless synchrony: 55% body language, 38% voice tone and 7% words—the three "V's."

Maybe you're thinking, *But won't other people notice that I'm copying their behavior?* Actually, they won't, unless the copying is blatant. Remember, your movements must be subtle and respectful. If someone sticks a finger in his ear and you do the same, then yes, he'll probably notice that. But when a person is focused on a conversation, he or she will not pick up on subtle synchronizing.

Particular gestures. Hand and arm movements are especially easy and natural to synchronize by matching and mirroring. Some folks raise their shoulders when they talk; others wave their hands around as they express themselves. Do whatever they do. If you find it uncomfortable at first, then go at it a little at a time until with practice you become an expert synchronizer. Just the fact that you're noticing these different types of gestures is a big step in the direction of making people like you in 90 seconds or less.

Body posture. Overall posture is known as the attitude of the body. It shows how people present themselves and is a good indicator of emotional state. That is why we sometimes refer to it as "adopting a posture." When you can accurately adopt a person's posture, you can get a fair idea of how he or she feels.

Overall body movements. Whether it's a job interview or striking up a conversation at the museum fundraiser, observe the person's overall body movements, then gently mirror or match them. If he has a leg crossed, then cross a leg; if he's leaning against the grand piano, do it, too. If she's sitting sideways on the banquette, sit sideways; if she's standing with her hands on her hips, do the same. Body movements like leaning, walking and turning are easily synchronized.

Head tilts and nods. These are the simplest movements to synchronize. Fashion photographers know that most of the "feel" of a terrific cover shot comes from the "innuendo" created by subtle tilts and nods of the head. Sure, the face is important, but it's the angles that carry the message. Pay close attention to them. Most good physicians and therapists find that they synchronize tilts and nods without giving it a second thought. It says "I hear you, I see what you're saying and I feel for you."

Facial expressions. Along with tilts and nods, synchronized facial expressions show agreement and understanding. They come naturally. When he smiles at you, your natural inclination is to smile back. When she shows wide-eyed surprise, give it back to her. Look around at the next luncheon or dinner you attend, and notice how those with the deepest rapport are doing it all the time. It's an easy and natural, surefire way to make someone like you in 90 seconds or less. You can match the same amount and same style of eye contact. It may be fleeting, or direct or coy; whatever it is, pick up on it and return it in the same way.

Breathing. Pay attention to breathing. Is it fast or slow? Is it high in the chest, low in the chest or from the abdomen? You can usually tell how people are breathing by watching their shoulders or the folds in their clothing. Synchronizing with their breathing can be soothing and comforting to them.

An Exercise in Synchrony

In and Out of Sync

For this exercise, you will need two other people: A and B. A is the first to do the actions; B synchronizes with A's actions. You start off as the director.

Sitting, standing or walking, A and B converse casually about anything they want. A makes a point of moving about enough to give B some body movements and gestures to synchronize. After about a minute, tell them to break synchrony. At this point, B deliberately mismatches A's movements. After another minute or so, instruct B to get into sync again. Then, after another minute, get them to break once more. Finally, have them get back in sync before finishing.

Now switch places with A or B. Keep rotating so that each one of you assumes a different role in the exercise. Compare notes at the end of each rotation. The comments will most likely be similar to these: "When I broke synchronization, it was as if a huge wall had been erected between us" and "When we stopped synchronizing, the level of trust plummeted."

You can also try this out on your own. Synchronize someone for a couple of minutes, then deliberately mismatch his or her movements for one minute ➡️ before getting back into synchrony again. Go in and out at will and notice the difference; it will be tangible.

Leading

When you're sitting and talking with a friend, one of you might cross a leg and the other might do the same without thinking. This means that one of you is following the other's lead, which is a sure sign that the two of you are in rapport.

As you quickly become proficient at synchronizing, you can test to find out just how well your rapport is going. After three or four minutes, regardless of what has gone before and without the other person being aware of what you're doing, make a subtle move that's independent of your synchronizing—lean back or cross your arms and perhaps tilt your head. If the other person follows, then you are synchronized and have rapport and the other person is now subconsciously following *your* lead. If you tilt your head, she tilts hers. If you cross your legs, he crosses his. Just change what you're doing—make a movement, alter your vocal tone—and observe whether the other person matches or mirrors you. This way you can check to see if you are in rapport. If the other person doesn't follow your lead, go back to synchronizing his or her movements for a few minutes and try again until it works.

I teach volunteers who sit with cancer patients how to have rapport with those in their care. This is the first thing I stress. Breathe in and out with them. Then, when you speak, you're doing it on their "out" breath, and this has a very calming effect.

Rhythms. The same rule applies for anything rhythmic. If she taps her foot, tap your pencil; if he nods his head, pat your thigh. In the right circumstances and with judicious application, this works well as long as it is beyond conscious awareness. If not, the next sound you hear may be the door slamming shut—or worse. Just use common sense and discretion.

Synchronizing Voice

Voice accounts for 38% of face-to-face communication. It reflects how a person is feeling; in other words, his or her attitude. People who are confused will *sound* confused, and people with a curious attitude will *sound* curious. You can learn to synchronize these sounds.

Tone. Notice the emotions conveyed by the tone of voice. Tune in to these emotions, get a feel for them and use the same tone.

Volume. Does the other person speak in a quiet voice or a loud voice? The value of synchronizing volume is not so much in doing it, but more in what can happen if you *don't* do it. If you are naturally loud and excitable and you meet someone who is more soft-spoken and reserved, it goes without saying that the other person would feel much more at ease with someone who spoke in the same tender tones. Conversely, a jovial, back-slapping loudmouth would surely find lots of common ground with someone who radiated a comparable degree of exuberance.

Speed. Does the other person speak quickly or slowly? A thoughtful, slow-speaking individual can be completely unsettled or flummoxed by a speed talker, just as much as a slow, ponderous talker can drive a quick thinker to the point of distraction. Talking at the same speed as someone else makes as much sense as walking at the same speed.

Pitch. Does the voice go up and down? Voice pitch is one way to change someone's energy level. When you raise pitch and volume, you become more excited. When you lower them, you become calmer, right down to the intimacy of a whisper.

Rhythm. Is the voice flowing or disjointed? Some people have a melodic way of speaking, while others have a more pragmatic, methodical output.

Words. There is yet one more powerful area we can synchronize, and that is the use of a person's preferred words. We will be covering this fascinating world in Chapter 9.

Synchronizing allows you to deeply identify with other people and get a better understanding of where they're coming from. Practice synchronization in all your activities, whether you're in an interview, at a bus stop, dealing with your children, calming an unhappy customer, or talking to the teller at the bank, your yoga instructor, the barman at the pub. You're not likely to run out of partners. Make it a part of your life for the next few days until you are competent without trying—until it becomes second nature.

The
Secrets of
Communication

Part Three

7

It's Not All Talk—It's Listening, Too

Well, this is it! You've just introduced yourself to someone new. You remembered to open your body language and keep your body, voice tone and words all saying the same thing. You were first with the eye contact and first with the smile. You introduced yourself, and miracle of miracles—three seconds have gone by and you can still remember the other person's name. You've begun synchronizing, and you feel confident that rapport is building. But now what?

It's conversation time! Conversation is one very significant way to build rapport and forge the bonds of friendship. It comes in two equally important parts: talking and listening. Or, as you'll soon see, asking questions and actively listening.

You may have found yourself in a situation where you wanted to talk to someone but suddenly felt tongue-tied and self-conscious about doing so. Or maybe you've felt your stomach sink as you take your seat on an airplane next to some interesting-looking person and can't think of a way to start talking without feeling self-conscious. *What will they think of me? Am I boring? Am I intruding?* And most important: *How shall I start?*

The idea is to get the other person talking, then find out what matters to him or her and synchronize yourself accordingly. This is the realm of small talk, the hunting ground for rapport. It is here that you will search for common interests and other stepping-stones to rapport. While big talk is serious stuff like nuclear disarmament and politics, small talk is everything else: your personal Website, renovating the bathroom, a speeding ticket or the color of your cousin Marisa's new sports car.

Stop Talking and Start Asking!

Conversation is how we open other people up to see what's inside, to deliver a message or both. And questions are the spark plugs of conversation. Be aware, however, that there are two types of questions: those that open people up and those that close them down. Questions work with incredible ease and the results are virtually guaranteed, so be sure you know which is which.

Here's the difference. Open questions request an explanation and thus require the other person to do the talking. Closed questions elicit a "yes" or "no" response. The problem with closed questions is that once you've been given a response, you're back where you started— and you'll have to think of another question to maintain some semblance of conversation.

A simple formula for striking up a conversation: begin with a statement about the location or occasion, then ask an open question.

It's a good idea to precede an open question with an opening statement. The best type of rapport-inducing statement is one linked to something you already have in common with the other person: the meeting or party you're attending, some fascinating current event—even the weather will do in a pinch! We call this a location/ occasion statement. Examples include: "What an elegant room." "Look at all that food." "It was a wonderful service." "My wife knows a few of your piano pieces by heart." "He never knew what hit him." That sort of thing.

Next comes the open question: "Where do you think those vases came from?" "How well did you know him?" The very fact that your question is open will guarantee that you quickly receive free information.

Use opening-up words. Good conversation is like a leisurely game of tennis with the words being pitched back and forth for as long as there is mutual interest.

When the words go off the court, it's time to serve again. An open question is the equivalent of a well-aimed serve.

Open questions begin with one of six conversation-generating words: *Who? When? What? Why? Where? How?* These words invite an explanation, an opinion or a feeling: "How do you know that?" "Who told you?" "Where do you think this information comes from?" "When did you come to that conclusion?" "Why should I be interested?" "What good do these words do?" They assist us in establishing rapport and making connections because they oblige the other person to start talking and begin opening up.

You can boost these conversation generators by adding sensory-specific verbs: see, tell and feel. In doing this, you're asking the person to go into his or her imagination and bring out something personal to show you. "Where do you *see* yourself by this time next year?" "*Tell* me why you decided on Bali for your vacation." "How do you *feel* about calamari?"

Avoid closing-down words. These words will have you playing tennis all on your own against a brick wall. The opposite of opening-up words are these interrogatives: Are you . . . ? Do you . . . ? Have you . . . ?

In other words, any questioning forms of the verbs "to be," "to have" and "to do" will close off your chances of rapport-inducing conversation. They elicit a one-word reply: "yes" or "no." Then what? You have to ask another question. You're going nowhere:

"Are you sure?"

"Yes."

"Do you come here often?"

"No."

"Have you ever thought how wonderful it would be to just drop everything and go bungee jumping in the middle of the afternoon?"

"Yes."

"Did you realize that no matter how long and interesting you make your questions, if they begin with closing-down words you're more than likely going to end up with a one-word answer?"

"Oh."

For one whole day, do nothing but ask questions and answer questions with a question. For variety, ask only open questions. You'll soon get the idea.

In fairness, closing-down words do have their place—police, customs officials and certain other regulators of the people are taught to use them to get "straight" answers. However, I'd like to remind any of you who have had the pleasure of being on the receiving end of this type of "conversation" that it probably didn't make you like the person in 90 seconds or less!

Chance Encounters

There are times when you find yourself suddenly thrust into the presence of someone who's just too good to pass up. These delicious moments seem to coincide with the exact second that your brain freezes over and you go gaga: *Help, what do I say? What do I do? Where shall I look? What will people think?* Keep going with this line of self-questioning and you'll get the sweats, a palpitating heart, a beet-red face and goofy body language.

The easiest of these situations is when the two of you are thrust together: sitting next to each other on a train, plane or bus; riding in an elevator; waiting in a Laundromat or the lobby of a hotel; working in adjacent booths at a trade show; or checking out the cantaloupes to see if they're ripe at your local supermarket. In situations such as these, you already have quite a bit in common with which to work.

"Hi," "Hello" and "Good morning," accompanied by a smile, are all good ways to begin and a great way to get feedback. A returned smile is a good indication that you're on the right track. Keep it simple and unimposing; keep it courteous, happy and light. Don't get too close and personal right up front, or you might get excluded. You want people to say to their friends, "I met this really nice guy this morning," not "This disgusting pervert tried to hit on me."

Once you're sure the other person is responding favorably to the interaction, you can try some more specific opening lines. Not surprisingly, an opening line works better if it's an open question, but you may not always be able to find one that sounds natural. Sometimes you might have to start with a closed question or a location/occasion statement: "Do you know what time this bank closes today?" or "Phew, that's quite a storm." So make sure you have an open question ready for the follow-up in case all you get in response is a yes or no.

Below are some examples of "openers" to try once you've said hello or exchanged smiles. *Precede them all with a location/occasion statement.*

Anywhere

Where are you from?

I've never been there. What's it like?

How did you end up here?

On a train, plane or bus

How long are you going to be in Duluth/Stratford/Majorca?

Where are you from?

Have you always lived there? *If yes, try:* If I only had three hours to spend there, what should I see? *If no, then:* So where else have you lived?

How long will you be traveling for?

What do you think of Amtrak/Alitalia/these new Greyhound buses?

An interesting aside: When meeting someone for the first time, North Americans tend to ask, "What do you do?" whereas Europeans prefer "Where are you from?"

At the supermarket

If you're both standing in the fresh-fish line, staring at a pasta display or checking out avocados, you already have something in common.

How can you figure out if there are enough mussels in that bag for two people?

Can you tell me the difference between fresh pasta and the stuff in a box?

How can I tell if these are ripe?

Do you know where they keep the bags for the produce?

Have you ever tried this kind of sauce/frozen dessert/ mushroom before? *If yes, then:* How does it taste?/What is it like? *If no:* Is there another kind that you'd recommend?

How long would you cook a chicken this big?

I forgot to pick up some pickled octopus. Do you mind saving my place in line? *(This can be a good ice-breaker because you'll have an excuse to chat when you get back—if only about the octopus. Don't be gone long, though, or you'll risk annoying the other party.)*

In a hotel/motel lobby

Do you know where I can I get a map?

Have you stayed here before? *If yes:* What's it like? *If no:* Neither have I. So how did you come to choose this hotel?

Do you know this city at all? *If yes:* I've got only one day here. What do you think is a must-see? *If no:* So what brings you here?

At a convention

So where are you from?

What seminars have really grabbed you so far?

Do you know of any good restaurants outside of the hotel?

What did you think of the keynote speaker?

I'm going to get a coffee. Can I bring you one, too? *(Note: This last gambit works in countless situations as a way to sound out other people's level of interest. Usually, if they're not interested, they'll refuse your offer. If they accept, it often means they're willing to interact further.)*

At the Laundromat

Where can you get change around here?

Do you know where I can buy some postage stamps/ orange juice/cat food?

I'm going to get a coffee—can I bring you one, too? *(See above.)*

Does it really matter if you mix whites and colors?

In line at a movie/play/concert

Why did you pick this movie/play/concert?

So are you here to see Scarlett Johansson or Jonathan Rhys Meyers?

What did you think of the actor/author/performer's last film/play/CD?

At an exhibition/museum/trade show/county fair

Wow, what do you think of *that*?

Do you know where the vintage locomotives are?

What's your favorite event/display/ride so far?

Have you seen the giant pumpkin yet?

What ride would you suggest for someone who's afraid of heights?

Walking your dog or watching others walk theirs

He's adorable. What breed is he?

Great leash. Where did you get it?

So what are Chihuahuas really like, anyway?

Tip: Dog owners often end up socializing in public places, but don't get a dog unless you truly love animals!

Running into someone you're familiar with but have never plucked up the courage to talk to

Hi, I have a couple of tickets to a play/the circus/a concert, and I was wondering if you'd like to join me.

Hi, how nice to see you. Do you have time for a coffee?

In all of these situations, give the other person about three chances to interact. If after three questions or comments, he or she is clearly not responding enthusiastically, don't make a pest of yourself. Disentangle graciously by saying something simple like "Have a nice day," "Enjoy the show," "Enjoy the rest of your flight/trip/holiday," or whatever else is appropriate.

Free Information

It's actually easy to get free information from a stranger. This doesn't mean trying to learn someone's credit card number. What it means is learning the other person's name, interests, personal situation and more. As you will see, almost everybody is more than eager to give away this information if it's requested in the proper way.

In fact, people will tend to follow your lead in offering information. That's why you say your name first. And the more you give, the more they will, too.

If you say, "Hi, I'm Carlos," you're likely to get "Hi, I'm Paul."

If you start with "Hi, I'm Carlos García," you'll probably get "Hi, I'm Paul Tanaka."

And if you start with "Hi, I'm Carlos García, I'm a friend of Gail's," Paul will probably respond in a similar way: "Hi, I'm Paul Tanaka, and I work with Gail's husband."

When you add information tags to your name, people tend to respond to them because you've offered

Missed Cues

Mike arrives at the train station five minutes earlier than usual. It's a warm, misty morning, and there are about 20 other people on the platform. Most of the usual commuter crowd hasn't shown up yet. Mike tucks his newspaper under his arm, stirs his coffee with a plastic stirrer, then turns and flicks the stirrer successfully into the garbage can just behind him. As he moves back to his spot, he notices an auburn-haired young woman in a dark gray suit walking toward him. The woman stops about 10 feet away and sits on a bench. She carefully places her briefcase next to her and looks at her watch.

Mike casts a sideways glance at her, half closing his eyes and pursing his lips slightly in appreciation. He has found himself in this type of situation almost more often than he cares to remember: eyeing someone, longing to approach her and yet scared stiff at the prospect of making the connection. This time, he reminds himself that all he wants to do is start a conversation and get the young woman talking. His objective is not to have dinner with her tonight, not to go on holiday with her next Saturday, not to marry her by the end of the month. Just to say a few words to see if she wants to be friendly. He says the most obvious thing he can think of:

"Hi, do you mind if I sit here?"

The woman moves slightly to her left. "No, I don't mind," she murmurs, and Mike sits down.

"I haven't seen you at the station before," he says.

"This is my first day," she responds. "I'm starting work in an ad agency in town."

"The train gets pretty crowded at this time," Mike says, "but sometimes you can get a seat all the way."

Mike missed out on the free information. First day, ad agency. He should have picked up on this and used the conversation starters: where, what, why, when, who and how. What will you do there? Who are your main clients? Where is the agency? How did you get the job?

All right, let's try it from a woman's point of view:

Dorita, a website designer, is walking along the platform and sees an attractive if rather tired-looking man seated on a bench. She sits down beside him and notices he's reading the latest P.D. James mystery. P.D. James is her favorite author! He smiles at her as she sits, and knowing that they have the book in common, she smiles back.

But the man has gone back to reading. Dorita decides to plunge ahead.

"So, are you a P.D. James fan?"

"No," says the man. "Would you believe this is only the second mystery I've ever read?"

"Why is that?"

"I don't get much time for reading. I'm a resident at a hospital in the city."

"Well, I've read all her books. She's my favorite mystery author. Although I also like Dick Francis a lot."

What response can Dorita expect? The last thing out of her mouth is a series of statements, not questions. Dorita was on track with her second query, a "why" question, but then she ignored the free information the man had given her. Instead, she went on to talk about herself. If she'd been listening actively, she would have followed up with "Which hospital? A resident in what? Why did you pick that specialty?"—the "where," "what" and "why" that would have led to further conversation.

them the opportunity. If they don't respond, you've at least set up the situation. They know what you want, so give them a little encouragement. A raised eyebrow or a straight-out "And you?" will spur them on.

The idea is to respectfully gather as much information as possible by first offering information about yourself. You can use this information to broaden and deepen your rapport. This is something to get your teeth into. You are building momentum.

Active Listening

Listening is the other side of the conversation coin. As a good active listener, you must demonstrate that you're truly interested in the other person. The key to being an active listener lies in making a sincere effort to absorb what that person is saying and feeling.

Listening is different from hearing. You may *hear* a cello as part of an orchestra, but when you actively *listen* to that same cello, you're consciously focused on every note and absorbing the emotion.

Active listening is an active attempt to grasp and understand the facts and the underlying feelings of what is being said. It does not mean giving up your own opinions and feelings, but it does mean that you're there to empathize as much as possible. You can show how much you understand by giving the appropriate feedback. Listen with your eyes. Listen with your body. Nod your head. Look at the person. Keep your stance open and leaning. Encourage the other person verbally.

A distinction should be made here between the "parrot phrasing" school of listening and the "active" school. Parrot phrasing, or paraphrasing, involves giving back a more or less accurate version of what another person has just said.

Paul: "How have you been affected by the terrible weather we've been having?"

Cathy: "I love heat waves like this, but the man I'm seeing is threatening to move to Alaska without me and I think he's actually serious."

Paul: "Sounds like even though you love heat waves, you might have to move to Alaska if you want to stay with the man you're seeing."

The active school means responding to feelings:

Paul: "Sounds like you have some big decisions to make. Isn't it upsetting? How will you handle it?"

Simply put, with "parrot phrasing" it only sounds like you're listening, whereas with active listening people *feel* that you're listening and *feel* that you care.

Give spoken feedback. Get inside what the person is saying. This kind of feedback ranges from "Primal Sighs" and "International Grunts" like "Wow," "Aha," "Oh" and "Hm" (as you can imagine, these are difficult to demonstrate in a book) all the way to full-blown reactions like "Oh, really," "And then what?" and "You're not serious. So, what did she do?" Any kind of encouragement is welcome in a conversation; it keeps the ball rolling and shows that you're listening even though you're not saying much.

Give physical feedback. Use open, encouraging body language. Nod in agreement and use plenty of eye contact, but don't stare. Look away in thought (looking at your hands from time to time gives the impression of participation). If you're sitting in a chair, move to the front edge of your seat and look interested or enthusiastic. If you're standing, point your heart at the other person, nod from time to time, and look thoughtful, surprised or amused, or whatever your Really Useful Attitude inspires as an appropriate response to what the person is saying.

Give-and-Take

With practice, easy, natural conversation will become second nature to you. Here are some handy tips to work on as you develop and improve. First, as ever, assume a Really Useful Attitude. Be curious and show concern for others. Encourage them to talk with you by giving sincere feedback. Work toward finding common interests, goals and experiences, and communicate with enthusiasm, knowledge and interest.

Futility is doing the same thing over and over again and expecting different results.

At the same time, hold up your own end of the conversation. Speak clearly and deliberately. Slowing down your rate of speech will make you feel more confident; so will a low-key display of your sense of humor. It helps if you keep abreast of current events and the issues that affect our lives, so read a newspaper every day and be up to date on

Talking in Color

All conversation, big or small, is about painting word pictures of your experiences for other people. The more vividly you can convey these experiences, the more interesting people will think you are.

Here's a serviceable description of an everyday event:

"We stood in line for the streetcar for more than 20 minutes. I was so fed up."

There's nothing here to engage the other person's imagination. Instead of talking in black and white, learn to talk in color. Involve as many senses as you can in your conversation. Describe what things look like, what they sound like, how they make you feel and, if appropriate, what they smell and taste like:

"It was amazing standing there in silence among all those people. The rain had just stopped, and my collar was wet. The lights of the buildings were shining in the puddles, and the hot dog vendor behind us was wringing out . . ."

This is sensory-rich language, and the imagination—yours and theirs—revels in it.

what's going on in the world—the big issues, at least. In my seminars I have the participants prepare their own "10-second commercial." It's really just a way of telling others who you are and what you do in a few short sentences.

Be yourself. People will like you for who you are. The more you learn to relax, the easier this will become.

Handling Compliments

Accept all compliments graciously. Do it simply. Do it directly. Avoid the temptation to be too modest or self-effacing. The standard two-word response to a compliment is "Thank you." Then, if you choose to convert it into a conversation, go ahead and do so. A compliment with an interesting but less than gracious acknowledgment might go as follows:

"Marion, that's a beautifully tailored skirt."

"Thanks, I got it for six bucks down at the Salvation Army store."

A much simpler and rapport-enhancing response would be "Thank you, it's nice of you to notice." Such a compliment should also be acknowledged with eye contact, a smile and a pleasant tone of voice.

Compliments are fine as long as they are sincere. Exaggerated or false compliments destroy credibility and endanger whatever rapport has been established. Cheap flattery, tired clichés and patronizing remarks reek of insincerity and can be insulting. On the other hand, an honest expression of praise can reinforce self-confidence and even lift the rapport onto a more heart-felt, personal level.

If you notice something good or interesting about

Sound Effects

Your tone of voice tells other people how you're feeling, and a pleasing tonality can positively affect the way they respond to you. Pleasing tonality occurs when your voice comes from deep down in your body, from your abdomen. It is deep, rich and infectious, compared to a monotonous voice or high-pitched braying.

To improve your own tonality, practice breathing and speaking from your abdomen. "Belly breathing," which uses your lungs to the fullest, is the most calming and healthy way to breathe. You breathe more slowly and with less stress. Contrast this to chest breathing, which is the way about 60% of the population get their air. Chest breathing is panicky, fight-or-flight breathing—just a series of long ➡

someone, or a praiseworthy performance, then a compliment is in order. Avoid general words like "nice," "good" and "great." "Nice suit"—big deal! "Blue really suits you" sounds better. "You're such a good person" sounds like a buildup to being dumped. "You bring out the best in everyone"—now, that's a compliment.

Specific compliments usually come across as being more sincere than general compliments. "Great soup" won't stimulate your host or hostess as much as "Was pants. Naturally, if you breathe from your chest, you will speak from the chest.

Put the palm of one hand gently on your chest and the palm of the other gently on your abdomen. Practice breathing until the hand on your chest doesn't move in and out and the hand on your abdomen does. When you've got it, take away your hands and just keep breathing that way—for the rest of your life. You'll notice that when you get nervous or excited, your breathing will return to your chest. Be aware of this, and take it back down; you'll immediately feel calmer.

Repeat this exercise with your hands on the place where your voice originates. Move your voice from your chest to your abdomen. It should sound lower, richer and a little slower—which is exactly the way you want it to be for establishing instant rapport and making people like you in 90 seconds or less.

that the tiniest hint of fresh dill I just tasted? You've done it again!" If you're complimenting performance, take the trouble to go into detail. "You were wonderful today" is not half as powerful as "You handled that question about the nursing home without flinching. That was an impressive strategy."

Deliver your compliment the same way you do your greeting: open your heart and your body, look directly at the person, speak with a clear, enthusiastic voice, give specific praise and remember to give the person time to respond.

Avoiding the Pitfalls

Read the list of "don'ts" below. If you catch yourself doing any of them, you may have abandoned your Really Useful Attitude or chosen a useless attitude by mistake:

Don't interrupt, and don't end other people's sentences for them, no matter how enthusiastic or impatient you might be.

Take Dale Carnegie's advice. Don't complain, don't condemn and don't criticize.

Whenever possible, avoid giving one-word answers; they don't usually qualify as conversation, and they put a heavy strain on rapport. People who monopolize conversations also trample all over rapport because there is little or no room to find common ground. They just come off as being rude or boring.

There's nothing quite so disconcerting as talking to someone who is looking elsewhere. If this happens to you, excuse yourself as fast as possible. People who do this are incongruent and, frankly, just plain rude.

Finally, look out for bad breath and all the other nasty personal hygiene stuff. No excuses here. Dragon breath, BO and spinach in the teeth might not make you any less lovable in the eyes of your golden retriever, but they won't do anything for you at the office party.

Making Yourself Memorable

What good is meeting someone for the first time, creating a favorable impression and establishing rapport if two weeks later the person has forgotten you? It's like writing a terrific story on your computer and forgetting where you filed it. Give other people a reason to remember you, and they will. The mind delights in making connections.

You'll remember from Professor Mehrabian's work on believability that face-to-face communication was broken up into 55% the way we look, 38% the way we sound and 7% the actual words we use. Something similar holds true for memory. Other studies show that what people see has about three times as much impact as what they hear.

Ask yourself these questions: How can I stand out from the rest? Is there a persona or some little touch of style I can create for myself? All kinds of things can give you an image: a fresh cornflower worn in the lapel or discreet, very expensive frames for your eyeglasses; beautiful vests, impeccable shoes, a bow tie, Mario Batali's orange clogs; Julianne Moore's hair or Goldie Hawn's laugh.

A friend of mine works for a national chain of megastores that sells computers and stereos. "I used to spend half an hour explaining the features of a product," she told me, "and then the customer would go away to think about it. He would come back another

Lasting Impressions

Jill and Robin, two middle-aged ladies, are sitting across from each other at a table in a French restaurant. They're halfway through lunch when several people are shown to a table nearby. A young woman in the group recognizes Jill and lets out a gasp of delight. She was a student in one of Jill's classes several years ago.

After many hugs and exclamations, Jill turns to her lunch companion: "Robin, this is Edwina. She was one of my most wonderful students back in my days in Stratford. I'll never forget—she had these rituals for organizing herself and her work. Everything had its own special place and order at her desk. Sometimes she drove me crazy, but it always used to fascinate me how meticulous she was."

"Nice to meet you," Robin says, taking Edwina's hand.

"So tell me, Edwina, what are you doing these days?" Jill asks.

Edwina proceeds to tell Jill about her work as associate producer on a local TV show, and then adds: "There are quite a few of us there from school. Do you remember Suzanne Sparks?"

"No, I'm sorry, I can't quite picture her," Jill says, searching about with her eyes.

"You know, the one who always came to class in those crazy leather vests."

➡

"Oh yes, of course." Jill turns to Robin, including her in the picture. "Suzanne was a terrific painter. I believe she spoke Spanish and German, too. Does she still have that mop of spiky red hair?" she asks, turning back to Edwina.

"No. She's long and blond now, and she's our director of programming. And what about Toni?" Edwina continues. "She's at the station, too."

"Now, which one was Toni?" Jill asks.

"Toni March. She was always really friendly. Lived out in Malton." When Jill gives no sign of recognition, Edwina says: "She was such a hard worker."

"Sorry, dear, I can't quite place Toni. Who else?"

"Greg Cuddy. He's our sales manager."

"No! Not Greg with the nose ring?" Jill shakes her head in disbelief. "Greg Cuddy was such a nervous young man. He drove his mother's pickup truck everywhere. If memory serves me correctly, he ran a train-spotting site on the Internet. He published a newsletter and had people from . . ."

Jill invites Edwina to join them at their table, and her friends at the other table order lunch without her as the reminiscing continues.

The point of this story is that it's easy for Jill to recall her former students when her memory is triggered by an image. People are more likely to be remembered if they have some kind of handle—some kind of device that makes them stand out from the crowd.

113

day, go up to the first salesperson he saw and make the purchase. It didn't matter that he had my card or that I gave him so much time; the chances of his coming back to me personally were slim. Then I hit on a way to be memorable. Because I'm from Newfoundland, I tell customers to ask for the 'Newfie' when they come back or phone the store." In Canada, a "Newfie" is often the target of dumb, stereotypical jokes, but my friend used this verbal image to her advantage. It is a handle or, if you prefer, a container to hold and access a whole package of previously stored information.

Find something to set you apart from the rest. Give them something to remember you by.

8

Making Sense of Our Senses

On one level, we humans are not much more than mobile sensing devices. We see, hear, feel, smell and taste. And then we process the information gained through our senses into words, then thoughts, ideas, actions and habits (in that order), which in turn forms our personality. Every day, we experience the world through sensory input, and then we explain our experiences to ourselves and to others. That's it. We go to bed and get up the next day and experience all over again. This is how we evolve. Obviously this is a major oversimplification, but it's a good place to start.

There are basically two ways, or styles, of explaining our experiences using words. One positive, the other negative. Upon waking up in the morning and seeing that it's raining outside, an individual with a negative explanatory style might say, "Oh, heck, it's raining. It's going to be a lousy day," whereas someone with a positive style might say, "Hey, free car wash, and great for the garden." Given the same information, some people are very good at spotting problems while others are good at spotting opportunities. And so, our really useful, or useless, attitudes are triggered by pictures, sounds and feelings.

We can loosely categorize these responses into familiar mind-sets and patterns. In the 1970s Richard Bandler and John Grinder, the founders of Neuro-Linguistic Programming, noticed in their early work with clients that people could be roughly divided into three types, depending on how they filtered the world through their senses. They called these types Visual, Auditory and Kinesthetic. Let's say three students go to a rock concert. Judy is primarily Visual, Phyllis is Auditory and Alex is Kinesthetic. When they later describe their experience to their friends, Judy will paint word pictures to tell what the concert looked like: "Oh, wow, you should have seen it—all these people jumping about and the singer ripped his pants and his toupee flew off!" Phyllis will say what the concert sounded like: "The music was incredible. The beat was deafening; everyone was yelling and singing along. You should have heard it. It was a real screamer!" Alex, who relates to feelings and touch, will describe what it felt like: "Oh man, you could just feel the energy. The place was packed. We could hardly move, and when they played 'Blue Rodeo' the whole place erupted."

In other words, Visuals tend to use picture words, Auditories choose sound words and Kinesthetics favor physical words.

What we are talking about here is a new dimension of synchrony and rapport. This chapter will go beyond attitude, body language and voice tone to the very way our senses take in and literally make sense of the world around us.

Visual, Auditory or Kinesthetic?

Because we receive our information from the outside primarily in pictures, sounds and feelings, these are the three ways in which we can be inspired: by something we see externally, or internally in our mind's eye as an image or a vision; by something we hear either externally or emanating from that little voice inside; or by something we feel or touch. Usually it's a combination of these experiences that helps us interpret the outside world, but one of these three senses—sight, sound or touch—tends to dominate the other two.

To the untrained eye (or ear), all of us look, sound and feel just like ordinary folks; however, to the trained person there are subtle but important differences. As you might imagine, an individual who gives primary importance to the way things look will be concerned with and influenced by appearances. Similarly, someone to whom sound is important will respond to the way things sound, and a person who experiences the world through physical sensations will be concerned with the way things feel, both internally and externally, through touch.

Last year I was listening to two politicians being interviewed on the radio. They were both thinking of running for the leadership of their party. When the interviewer asked them to "voice their plans," one said, quite thoughtfully, "I'm leaning heavily toward giving it a shot." The much quicker response from the other man was "Now that we have a clearer view of the future, I can see the possibilities." The interviewer responded, "Sounds like you're both ready to announce your intentions."

What do you reckon? Can you grasp the distinction? The interviewer, using phrases like "voice your plans" and "announce your intentions," was probably Auditory. (In all fairness, that would be natural language to use on the radio, but still a surprising number of radio hosts turn out to be Auditory.) The first aspiring leader used physical language—"lean heavily," "give it a shot"—and spoke deliberately, indicating a Kinesthetic inclination. The second hopeful candidate had "a clearer view" and could "see the possibilities," and therefore came across as pretty Visual to me.

Of course, no one is totally Visual, utterly Auditory or 100% Kinesthetic. Naturally, we are a mixture of all three. Yet, in every person, one of these systems (rather like left- or right-handedness) dominates the other two.

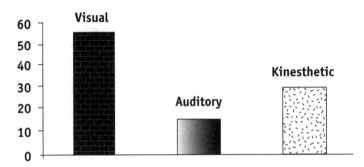

Studies have shown that as many as 55% of all people in our culture are motivated primarily by what they see (Visual), 15% by what they hear (Auditory) and 30% by physical sensation (Kinesthetic).

Take the self-test on pages 120–123, and you'll begin to see why you connect easily with some people when you first meet them but not at all with others, and why you feel as if you know certain people even though you've never seen them before. It comes down to natural sensory harmony. When two Visuals meet, they are familiar to each other because they see things the same way (this doesn't mean they agree) and express their experiences in the same way. The same goes for two Auditories or two Kinesthetics. On the other hand, if the person you meet sees, hears or feels the world in a different way from yours, you need to learn how to recognize that fact and how to adapt and tune in to his or her wavelength to

What's Your Favorite Sense?

Where would you place yourself among the Visuals, Auditories and Kinesthetics? Like many people, you'll probably say, "Oh, I'm a Visual, for sure." But you might be in for a big surprise. Take the following test to see how you tune in to the world. Choose only one answer from each question, and circle the letter next to your answer.

1) If only three rooms are left at a beach resort, I'll choose the room that offers
   a) An ocean view but lots of noise.
   b) Sounds of the ocean but no view.
   c) Comfort but lots of noise and no view.

2) When I have a problem,
   a) I look for alternatives.
   b) I talk about the problem.
   c) I rearrange the details.

3) When riding in a car, I want the inside to
   a) Look good.
   b) Sound quiet or powerful.
   c) Feel comfortable or secure.

➡

4) When I explain a concert or event I've just attended, I first
   a) Describe how it looked.
   b) Tell people how it sounded.
   c) Convey the feeling.

5) In my spare time, I most enjoy
   a) Watching TV or going to the movies.
   b) Reading or listening to music.
   c) Doing something physical (crafts/gardening) or playing a sport.

6) The one thing I personally believe everyone should experience in his or her lifetime is
   a) Sight.
   b) Sound.
   c) Feeling.

7) Of the following activities, I spend the most time indulging in
   a) Daydreaming.
   b) Listening to my thoughts.
   c) Picking up on my feelings.

8) When someone is trying to convince me of something,
   a) I want to see evidence or proof.
   b) I talk myself through it.
   c) I trust my intuition.

9) I usually speak and think
   a) Quickly.
   b) Moderately.
   c) Slowly.

10) I normally breathe from
    a) High in my chest.
    b) Low in my chest.
    c) My belly.

11) When finding my way around an unfamiliar city,
    a) I use a map.
    b) I ask for directions.
    c) I trust my intuition.

12) When I choose clothes, it is most important
    to me that
    a) I look immaculate.
    b) I make a personal statement
       about my personality.
    c) I feel comfortable.

13) When I choose a restaurant, my main
    concern is that
    a) It look impressive.
    b) I can hear myself talk.
    c) I will be comfortable.

14) I make decisions
   a) Quickly.
   b) Moderately.
   c) Slowly.

Tally:
a's = _____
b's = _____
c's = _____

a) is Visual, b) is Auditory and c) is Kinesthetic. The higher the number in each category, the stronger the tendency.

By taking this test, not only will you now have a strong indication of how your three main senses stack up, but you'll also begin to understand how people can have differing priorities. However, there are many variables at work here, not the least of which is that you already knew the purpose of the test before you took it. In my seminars, I generally have people complete this test before they realize its significance.

Try it on a few friends and see how they fare. Use their results to further your insight into being able to recognize sensory preferences.

establish rapport that can lead to a meaningful friendship or relationship.

To give you an idea of how sensory preferences impact on our day-to-day life, let me tell you about my own situation. I am Auditory and my wife is Kinesthetic. If we have a falling out, Wendy knows to connect to me in my "language," with Auditory words. She gets my immediate attention by saying, "Nick, you're not listening to me. You're not hearing a word I'm saying." If she were to say, "Can't you see what I'm saying" or, even worse, "Can't you see how that makes me feel?" the truth is, no, I could not.

Sure, I make the obvious intellectual connection, but I have to stop and think about it; my brain has to take the extra step of translating her language into something I can relate to. When she sends a message on my Auditory wavelength, she makes a direct connection—fast.

Conversely, if I want to connect directly to her sensibilities, I say, "I know how you feel when that happens." In other words, I use a touchy-feely, Kinesthetic approach. Simple, yet extraordinarily effective.

Tuning In to Sensory Preferences

What do sensory types have to do with making people like you in 90 seconds or less? More than you might expect. When you can figure out other people's sensory preferences, you can communicate on

Metaphorically Speaking

The words "I have scoured the four corners of the earth" tell a lot more than "I've looked everywhere"; they force the connection to scrutiny, diligence, detail, determination and more. They also easily involve sight, sound and feeling, and this is why metaphors appeal simultaneously to Visuals, Auditories and Kinesthetics. Visuals can picture them, Auditories can hear them and Kinesthetics can get a feel for what's happening.

Metaphors are containers for ideas. They link our internal imagination to external reality. We use metaphors regularly, often unconsciously, to explain our thinking. We also use them to make things more interesting. Parables, fables, storytelling and anecdotes are some of the oldest and most powerful communication tools we have, and their metaphorical aspects are effective in virtually every setting. They fire up the imagination and appeal to all the senses.

In short, metaphors help to make understanding easier, quicker and richer.

their wavelength. If you want to better relate to your spouse, win a judge over to your side of an argument, make that sale, land that job or impress somebody at a party, recognizing Visual, Auditory and Kinesthetic people can be invaluable.

The day after one of my seminars, I received an excited phone call from a woman who had been sitting in the audience. Her name was Barbara, and she owned a flooring store.

"It's incredible!" she said. "It's nine-thirty, we've been open for an hour and I've just sold to my fifth out of five customers. I've never done that before!

"This is perfect for my business," she continued, referring to my lecture on figuring out the Visual, Auditory and Kinesthetic people we come across in the course of our daily adventures. "The first four sales were probably normal, even though I was aware of what I'd learned. But the fifth . . . This lady came into the shop dragging her husband along with her. It was obvious that he didn't want to be there. I figured out immediately that he was a feeler, a Kinesthetic, and within 30 seconds I had him on his hands and knees feeling the carpet. And they bought it.

"I just knew that if I'd said to him, 'Imagine how this will look in your house,' he couldn't do that because he's not Visual. Or if I'd said, 'You'll discover just how quiet it'll be when your kids run around on it,' he wouldn't connect to that, either, because he doesn't think that way—he's not Auditory. I knew by the way he dressed and moved and spoke that he was Kinesthetic, so I said, 'Just feel it.' And he did. Just like that. He got down on the floor and felt it."

Find out what you're getting. Change what you do until you get what you want. These are the "F" and "C" in our KFC. Figure out which sense a person relies on most and change your approach to take this into consideration.

If you're not sure how to handle a situation, don't worry. Be prepared to include all three preferences in your approach. Look good for the Visuals; after all, they make up over half the people you're likely to see during your day. Sound good; develop your pleasing tonality for the Auditories to whom you'll be speaking. And be sensitive and flexible for the Kinesthetic folk you'll be bumping into. And, of course, if you're dealing with a group, the same thing applies. Your group will be made up of all three categories, and you'll want to appeal to all of them.

Above all, remember that the ability to tune in to the way other people experience the world can be one of the most important discoveries of your life.

A few months ago I gave the opening address at a home builders' convention. During my talk, I used role-playing (with me playing all the roles) to illustrate some of the behavioral differences that Visual, Auditory and Kinesthetic people display in face-to-face communication. At the end of the talk, a big, tough-looking but well-

Sights and Sounds

Despite the good Colombian coffee and fresh croissants, the O'Connors are not enjoying a very pleasant breakfast.

"It's a bright yellow Maserati!" exclaims John. "It's gorgeous! Can't you just picture the two of us blazing down the highway to the coast?"

"Actually, I can't," says Lizzie icily. "All I can hear are the monthly car bills dropping through our mail slot. I don't think you ever listen when I tell you we have more important things to spend money on . . ."

John stomps out of the house in a rage, but that evening, after leaving work, he buys a luxurious, multicolor silk scarf for Lizzie in an attempt to win her over. Arriving home, he finds her in the living room and hands her the exquisitely wrapped box.

"And what is this for?" Lizzie asks distantly as she removes the scarf from its box. "What's the occasion?"

"Why, it's just to show how much I love you!" protests John, feeling rejected.

"A scarf doesn't tell me anything!" Lizzie snaps. She walks crisply out of the room.

John slumps down on the couch, slowly winding the expensive scarf around his hand and tightening it until his fingers throb with pain.

➡

What happened here? John is Visual. He makes sense of the world primarily through what he sees: the yellow Maserati, his "picture" of them in the car, the multihued scarf. Lizzie is Auditory. She hears the car bills dropping through the mail slot; she doesn't think John "listens" when she "tells" him something.

Can this marriage (or at least the hoped-for Maserati purchase) be saved? You bet. A pair of concert tickets to Lizzie's favorite band—something that appeals to her ears—would sound much better to her. Here's how John could have handled it had he been more sensitive to the way Lizzie hears the world:

"I'm really sorry, Lizzie," declares John in a soft, pleasant voice (after giving her the tickets). He proceeds to use some "auditory" words with his wife. "I'll tell you what—let's put some harmony back in this house and talk it through a bit. Does that sound okay to you?"

Lizzie nods, taking in the suddenly more acceptable words and the meaning they convey.

"Have I told you how the Maserati purrs like a kitten and shifts so quietly you can barely hear it?" John asks sweetly. "And wait until we discuss the surprisingly reasonable payments."

"Oh, I finally see the picture you're painting, John," says his wife. "It's all so clear to me now!"

groomed man pulled me to one side. He was very emotional and looked like he was on the verge of tears. Shaking his head from side to side, he began, "I don't know what to say. I'm leaving right now to go to my son's school and give him a hug." He was choking up. "For years, I've been furious with him. When I talk to him, he turns his head away and doesn't look at me. It drives me crazy, and I yell at him, 'Look at me when I'm talking!' He hardly ever looks me straight in the eye when I'm giving him instructions. From everything you've said, you've made me realize that he's Auditory, and he's not ignoring me when he looks away. He's turning his ear toward me so he can concentrate. And me, I'm Visual, I need eye contact." He pumped my hand and left.

It's amazing. Things like this go on right under our noses every day of our lives and we never realized—until now, that is.

9

Spotting Sensory Preferences

Recognizing which senses other people rely on to experience the world and then using this information in your dealings with others—whether personal, professional or social—can have a profound effect upon how they respond to you. This chapter deals with picking up the initial cues that other people give us without knowing it. Whether Visual, Auditory or Kinesthetic, their signals are there for us to interpret and utilize in establishing rapport.

In the question period at the end of one of my seminars, a middle-aged woman in the second row asked slowly, "Do you feel that it's hard to put your finger on what a person's sensory preference is?" This delightful woman wore a big, comfortable knit coat and was twiddling her finger slowly through her hair as she spoke. I thanked her for the question and immediately asked her not to move. Obviously a very good-natured person, she froze in position. "I'm going to ask you to repeat your question in exactly the same way," I said to her. "But I want the rest of the audience to observe. Is that okay?" She nodded, paused and repeated her question, complete with hair twiddling. There was a collective smile from the other people in the audience as they understood what they had just witnessed. Then the lady herself looked up toward the top of her head and chuckled.

Her choice of the words "feel," "hard" and "put your finger on," her easy way of speaking, her comfortable coat, her slightly full figure and her habit of playing with her hair were quite the giveaways. She had dropped enough clues to give the whole audience a strong indication as to what this woman's sensory preference might be.

You weren't there, but what sense do you think she most relies on?

You're right on if you said Kinesthetic.

Sensory Preference Profiles

Each group displays subtle differences in physical and mental makeup. These are definitely not hard-and-fast distinctions. They are simply indicators. Visuals, Auditories and Kinesthetics can come in all shapes and sizes. We are dealing with people here, unique individuals with unlimited beliefs and values, opinions and talents, shades and sparkles, innuendos and dreams. Each one is different; yet, deep down, there are fundamental similarities. Find a person who strongly favors one sense in a number of the areas discussed in this chapter, and chances are that he or she will be signaling a personal sensory preference.

A quick tip:
Visuals usually talk very fast.
Kinesthetics tend to talk slowly.
Auditories fall somewhere in between.

As you become aware of the differences among these three groups of people, Visual, Auditory and Kinesthetic, what seems subtle at first will become more and more obvious to you.

Perhaps you've had the experience of buying a new car. Let's say you bought a nifty little blue Prius. Very unique? Not quite. Suddenly blue Priuses are everywhere. Whereas before you only noticed them once in a great while, you start to see them all over the place. Of course, these cars were there all the time—they just held no interest for you.

When you become more accomplished at distinguishing one person from another, the same thing will happen. The distinctions will reveal themselves before your eyes. And yet they've been there all the time.

TV Giveaways

TV talk shows are a great place to brush up on your preference-spotting talents. The late shows, where everyone tends to overdress, are usually not the best venues for this exercise. Far better are the interview shows with hosts like Charlie Rose or Larry King or local talk shows where people are more themselves.

Turn down the volume and try to figure out—through physical appearance, hand gestures, eye movements and clothing—whether the person is a V, an A or a K. Then turn up the volume and listen to the words, the pace of speech and the tonality of the voice.

You can do the same with radio interviews. Concentrate on the words. Radio talk shows are a mine of information about sensory preferences. You can practice while you're stuck in traffic.

Take it slowly. Have fun.

Visuals

Visual people care a lot about how things look. They need to see proof, or evidence, before they take anything seriously. Being visualizers, they think in pictures and wave their hands around, sometimes touching their pictures when talking. Pictures come quickly into their mind's eye, so they think clearly; this makes them the fast talkers among us. Sometimes they are the ones with the monotonous voices. Visuals frequently look up to the left and right when they speak. When it comes to their wardrobe, they tend to be snappy, impeccable dressers who put a lot of work into looking good and surrounding themselves with good-looking stuff. Physically, because they are concerned with appearances, they aim to be trim and tidy. When they stand and sit, their body and head will usually be upright.

You will find Visuals working where confident, fast decisions are needed or where specific procedures are to be followed. They want to have control because they probably have some kind of vision of how things should be. Many—but definitely not all—visual artists fall into this category.

Auditories

Auditory people respond emotionally to the quality of sound. They enjoy the spoken word and love conversation—but things must sound right for them to tune in and give their attention. They have fluid, melodic, sensitive, persuasive, expressive voices. "Audis" move their eyes from side to side as they talk and gesture somewhat less than Visuals; but when they do, it's from side to side, like their eye movements. When it comes to clothes, they *think* they are snappy dressers. They like to make a statement with their clothing—and sometimes they don't quite make it. Physically, they are somewhere in between the trim Visuals and the comfortable Kinesthetics.

Audis work where words and sound are the currency. Many broadcasters, teachers, lawyers, counselors and writers are Auditory.

Kinesthetics

For our sensitive "Kinos," things have to be solid, well constructed and right-feeling in order for them to go along. They have lower, easygoing voices and gestures. Some Kinesthetics have been known to speak unbelievably slowly and add all sorts of unnecessary details that can drive Visuals and Auditories to the point of wanting to yell, "*Please,* for heaven's sake, get to the point!" That's just the way many of them are. The fact of the matter is that it takes longer to put feelings into words than it does to translate pictures or sounds into words. When they speak, Kinos will look down, toward their feelings. They enjoy the way things feel. They like textured clothing with quiet tones. Any man with permanent facial hair may well be Kinesthetic. You'll find Kinos in hands-on positions: plumbers, electricians, carpenters, product salespeople and workers in the arts, medicine and the food business.

Physically, there are two types of Kinos: in one group are the athletes, dancers, emergency services and trades folk, the superfit types for whom the physicality

Pushing for More

 This simple technique has proved helpful in determining a person's sensory preference. Start by asking a couple of nonspecific questions: "Do you live in the city or out in the suburbs?" followed up, after the response, by "Do you like it?"

If the answer is yes, ask, "What do you like most about it?" (If the answer is no, follow with "What don't you like about it?")

As the reasons are given, push for more. Expanding on answers like "Well, for one thing, it's peaceful" can be encouraged by the question "What else?" And don't stop there. Pursue your line of questioning until you have enough verbal cues to get a handle on the person's favorite sense.

of touch and contact are paramount; in the other group are the sensitive, laid-back, down-to-earth, bighearted types who may have a higher proportion of heavier bodies among their number.

Matches and Mismatches

You can probably see for yourself that the chances of establishing a loving relationship with someone "like" you are high. But is this always a good idea? Yes and no. If you want to spend your life with someone very much like you, then yes. But what if you want some spark and excitement?

I am frequently asked whether there is any validity in the age-old aphorism that opposites attract. The answer is yes, they most definitely do. But how? And what do they attract?

First let me say that this book is about establishing rapport and making people like you. If rapport and liking lead to friendship and romance, that's up to you. I like, trust and care about a lot of people, but they are not all my friends and they are definitely not my partners. Falling for someone romantically is more complex. To write my book *How to Make Someone Love You Forever in 90 Minutes or Less*, we questioned nearly 2,000 people whose relationships have lasted more than 20 years and are still vibrant. We found a simple pattern. I coined the term "Matched Opposites" because these great couples are a blend of "like attracts like," because they actually like each other, and "opposites attract," because there has to be an ongoing spark. Some of the "opposites" part can be seen in their patterns of sensory preferences. In this aspect, most were *complete opposites*.

You'll remember from the self-test in Chapter 8 that the tally at the end allowed you to rank your preferences. Let's use my own rating as an example. I ranked first A, then V and last K, or AVK. The complete opposite of my ranking would be KVA. Stack these side by side and they look like this:

A	**K**
V	**V**
K	**A**

This would give us opposites at the top, A and K, for spark and interest, but the same in the middle—in this case, V. The relationship is held together by the common visual link, a mutual subconscious sharing of the same wavelength. And the relationship is kept vital by the opposing A and K as primary personal sensory preferences.

My observation is that when two people "meet in the middle" and share a central sensory preference, whether Visual, Auditory or Kinesthetic, it is that bond that will get them through the rough times and add sparkle to the good times. Any shared sensory preferences, be they primary, secondary or tertiary, will work in the favor of the relationship when the going gets tough.

Verbal Cues

There are no fixed rules here, except that the people you meet will tend to reveal how they change their experiences into words by the types of words they favor. Listen for these words and take them into account when you set out to establish rapport.

Visual Words

A tendency to favor "picture" words and metaphors—
"if we look more clearly," "the difference was like night
and day"—may be a strong indication that the person
relies mainly on the visual sense.

For one entire day—from dawn to dusk—focus on
the Visual words and phrases that you hear in other people's vocabulary. Notice them until they appear as clear
as the three extremely visual words I just used in this
one sentence. The list of picturesque words below will
give you perspective and focus as you observe people
who scrutinize the world with their eyes. Then demonstrate how well you can use these Visual words. Make
the effort in your conversations with other people to
"talk in color" by painting word pictures. Describe your
experiences vividly so other people can "see" them.

analyze	colorful	focus
angle	conspicuous	foresee
appear	dark	fuzzy
aspect	diagram	glance
blind	dim view	glare
bright	dull	glimpse
brilliant	enlighten	glow
clarity	envision	hide
clear	examine	hindsight

Visual Talk

How do you see yourself?

It's a bit hazy right now.

I see what you're saying.

He's such a colorful character.

A sight for sore eyes.

Let's get some perspective.

We are a company with a vision.

We see eye to eye on the subject.

It's a bit vague.

Beyond a shadow of a doubt.

See you later.

Can you imagine?

Let me make this clear.

Can you shed some light on this?

We have a bright future.

illuminate	oversight	scrutinize
illusion	notice	show
imagine	peek	sketch
inspect	perception	staring
light	perspective	survey
looks great	picture	view
mental picture	plainly	vision
mind's eye	portray	vivid
obscure	reflect	watch
observe	reveal	witness
outlook	see	zoom in

Auditory Words

Tune in to Auditory words and phrases as people express themselves to one another. Call to mind and amplify all those harmonious discussions within your hearing range until you are well informed about how they sound. Listen to how these Auditory words just click into place! Open your ears to those who see and feel the world through their hearing. You'll get the message loud and clear.

announce	divulge	outspoken
articulate	earful	overtones
babble	earshot	phrase
blabbermouth	express yourself	proclaim
boom	gossip	pronounce
call (me)	harmonize	question
chime	hear	quiet
clang	hidden message	rasp
clash	hush	remark
click	idle talk	report
converse	inquire	resonate
crashing (bore)	listen	resounding
deaf	loud	roar
debate	manner of speaking	rumor
describe in detail	mention	say
discuss	noisy	scream

Auditory Talk

Sounds familiar.

Tell me more.

Does what he said ring a bell with you?

He gave a satisfactory account of himself.

At last we have harmony at home.

They granted me an audience.

She had me completely tongue-tied.

These colors are really loud.

I didn't like his tone of voice.

Let me tell you.

Tell me how.

She's a scream.

In a manner of speaking . . .

I want everybody in the room to voice an opinion.

He received thunderous applause.

That's as clear as a bell.

Hold your tongue!

shout	talk	utter
shrill	tell	vocal
silence	tinkling	well-informed
speak	tone	whine
speechless	tongue-tied	word-for-word
squawk	tune in/out	yell
state	unheard of	

Kinesthetic Words

The following physical words are the currency of the Kino. Tap into the emotions around you until you get a handle on how they flow. Overcome any and all stumbling blocks. Build a firm foundation on which you can base your own contact with other people. Use those concrete, touching words that move Kinesthetic people, thanks to their sensitivity to feelings.

bearable	grasp	push
boils down to	hand-in-hand	rush
break	handle	sensitive
catch on	hard	set
cold	heated	shallow
come to grips with	hold	sharp
concrete	hunch	shift
connect	hurt	shocking
dig	intuition	smooth operator
emotional	light-headed	softly
explore	make contact	solid
feel	motion	sort through
firm	muddled	squeeze
(go with the) flow	nail	stir
foundation	pain in the neck	strain
freeze	pressure	stress

Kinesthetic Talk

How do you feel about . . . ?

There were a few stumbling blocks.

I'll get in touch with her.

It slipped through the cracks.

I'm all shook up.

I'm not following you.

Let's sort things out.

Get a load of this!

Can you pull some strings?

She came to grips with the problem.

Get over it.

I can't handle the pressure.

He's a pain in the neck.

Stay in touch.

Hang in there.

I can't put my finger on anything concrete.

Start from scratch.

Walk me through the ceremony one more time.

I felt calm, cool and collected.

Let's explore the possibilities.

stretch	throw out	underhanded
structured	tied up	unfeeling
support	topsy-turvy	unravel
tap into	touch	unsettled
tension	unbearable	warm

Eye Cues

Over the years, I have shot more fashion magazine covers with more models in more countries than I can remember, and frequently the models' first language was not English. When all you have to work with is a face, neck and shoulders (and, of course, the extraordinary talents of hair, makeup and fashion stylists), you soon realize that, besides subtle tilts and leans, most of the "innuendo" suggested by this kind of close-up comes from facial expression—from the eyes and mouth. When you want a model to smile, you don't tell her to smile. You make her smile.

To initiate eye movements, there are a few code words that always seem to work in any language. When you want your subject to look up and to the side, it's enough to say, "Just dream," and up go the eyes to one side or the other. Words such as "secret" or "telephone" will send the eyes sideways toward the ears, and "sad," "romantic" or "thoughtful" will normally send the eyes down and to the left or right.

Once again, the originators of NLP had observed these phenomena of eye movements and codified them into an intriguing paradigm. On the basis of their findings, we can think of the human eyeball as a six-way switch that must be flicked into any one of six positions as it searches for information—each position activating a sense, sometimes to remember, sometimes to create an answer.

If you ask a man to tell you the color of his favorite shirt, you may see him look up and to his left as he pictures the shirt before he gives you an answer. Ask a woman to tell you what silk feels like, and chances are she'll look down and to her right as she remembers how silk feels in her mind. In other words, when asked a question, people often have to look away in order to generate the answer. The reason is quite simple: they are accessing their senses.

Keep your eye on the ball. Turn down the sound on your TV during an interview and watch the guest's eyes hunt about for answers to the interviewer's questions.

Before you read any further, go and ask someone a question. Without telegraphing your intent, look the person in the eye and ask a nonspecific question such as "What did you like most about your last holiday (or birthday or job)?" Then watch as the person's eyes dart off to get the information. This will give you a fairly good idea of how he or she stores and accesses information, i.e., as pictures, sounds or feelings. Consistent references to one sense are also an indication of sensory preference.

People who answer such questions while looking up to the left or right are most likely visualizing their answer. If they look left or right toward their ears, they are probably recalling sound information. If they look down to the left, they may well be accessing their feelings, and down to the right indicates some type of internal dialogue. Research has varying views as to the validity of these NLP eye cues, but I find them fairly accurate, and most importantly they lead to proactive eye contact for many people who are often too shy to look another person directly in the eye without discomfort.

Another valuable detail to be aware of here is that when we look to the left, we are *remembering* information, while looking the other way, to the right, means we are *constructing* it.

Keep in mind that when you converse with someone, there may be several mental activities going on at once. For example, a fellow asks a young woman, "Seen the latest Bruce Willis movie?" "Yes, I have," she says, going into her mind and picturing herself in the waiting line as she remembers. But at the same time she's having an internal dialogue: "What a boring twit. Am I judging too quickly? No, he's a bore. How can I dump him?" Then he says, "Wanna go out Saturday night?" Grasping for any excuse, she finally mutters, "Gosh, I can't, I have to, er, finish off a report for a Monday-morning

Brain Lock

Challenge a friend to answer the following questions without moving his eyes. Tell him to look directly at you at all times and to keep his eyeballs perfectly still. Then ask the first question:

"Do you like the house (apartment or whatever) you live in?"

Depending on whether he answers yes or no, ask this follow-up question:

"Quickly list six things you like (or don't like) about where you live."

Either your friend will be completely tongue-tied, or he'll find himself struggling to think of his answer. Searching for how things look, sound or feel without any eye movement is almost impossible. He'll be like a rabbit paralyzed in the grip of a car's headlights.

Hypnotists know that if they can stop your eyeballs from moving, you won't be able to think. A meditative state is easily accessed in the same way. Stare at a stationary spot with your eyes open, or place your attention in one spot—your forehead, for example—with your eyes closed. Provided you can keep your attention fixed, you will stop your inner dialogue and lose all sense of time.

deadline," her eyeballs darting off to the other side as she constructs a picture of herself at the kitchen table with her laptop.

Feeling a bit confused? Look at this diagram:

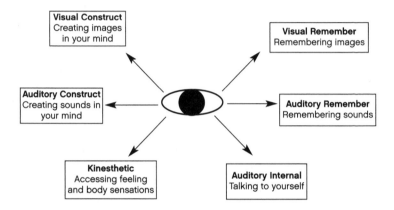

To avoid all confusion, imagine that this diagram is pasted on the forehead of the person you're facing. Don't worry about the person's left vs. your right; simply look at the diagram as if you were directly facing the other person. (In general, the directions apply to right-handed people, who make up 90% of the population.)

Incidentally, these actions are not the same as the movements your eyeballs make when you look around a room or across a landscape—they are totally independent of the requirements of the ability to see. Your eyeballs serve two purposes: 1) roving about to see what's going on; 2) activating sensory memory channels.

The Eyes Have It

Using the diagram on the facing page as a guide, pencil in the eyeball position you would expect to see in response to each question below.

Question	Eye Movement	System
What color socks are you wearing?		Visual Remember
How would you look in a green jacket?		Visual Construct
Can you remember what "Purple Haze" by Jimi Hendrix sounds like?		Auditory Remember
What would it sound like if it was played on the bagpipes?		Auditory Construct
What does sand feel like?		Kinesthetic
What are you telling yourself right now?		Auditory Internal (Talking to yourself)

Ingrid's Hard-Earned Vacation

It's her 40th birthday, and Ingrid has decided to treat herself to an all-inclusive holiday in Portugal. She's wandering through her neighborhood mall when she discovers a travel agency that she hasn't noticed before. There she meets Sheldon, who runs the place, and tells him of her exciting plans.

"I just feel I need to get away and pamper myself at long last!" Ingrid says to Sheldon as she sits down in a chair facing his desk. She smooths out her dress over her knees and looks down to her right. "I'm under so much pressure at work that I really need to unwind." Sighing, she crosses one leg over the other, leans forward and shakes her head slightly. "The tension at the office is eating me alive."

Sheldon is delighted. An obvious sale is sitting right there in front of him. He leans back in ➡

When you first begin looking for eye cues, people's eyes may appear to dart about randomly. All you need is a little practice at reading these movements.

Have fun, let it happen naturally and, above all, never tell anyone what you're doing. That would, quite rightly, make people self-conscious and embarrassed. Keep these skills to yourself.

his chair, opens his arms wide, then slaps his hands together sharply and smiles at Ingrid.

"Oh boy," he says, "have I got the dream vacation for you." He riffles through a pile of brochures on his desk. "Just feast your eyes on this!"

He hands Ingrid a colorful brochure plastered with the usual palm trees and bright blue skies, then continues his pitch without waiting for her reaction:

"Looks fantastic, eh? Check out the color of the water—brilliant turquoise! Look at these cute villas with their red-tiled roofs! And can't you just see yourself on that long white stretch of beach?" He looks up and to his right, just imagining the view.

Ingrid slides back in her chair, her heart sinking. Somehow, despite the gorgeous pictures in the brochure, despite Sidney's passionate descriptions, Portugal feels farther away than ever.

What's the problem?

➡

The Big Picture

The implications of verbal and eye cues discussed in this chapter are vitally important to anyone who wants to "connect" with other human beings and establish rapport by design. When you learn to recognize which "type" or "group" a new acquaintance belongs to,

You guessed it. Ingrid understands the world through her feelings. Look at her words: she "feels" that she wants to "pamper" herself; she longs to "unwind" from the "pressure" and "tension" at her office. Her language, intonation and gestures are a giveaway. She looks down toward her feelings. What counts most to Ingrid is the way things feel.

If Sheldon had been watching for cues, he would have gently led her toward a feeling of confidence and anticipation and warmth. "Okay, Ingrid," he would have said. "I follow you. I know what you mean about pressure, and I have just the place for you. I've actually been there myself. The sand is warm and soft, and, oh, the feel of those gentle waves as they break over you and around you! And the beds in these particular villas are amazingly comfortable and cool . . ." He would have accessed the same channel that Ingrid has been tuned in to for the past four decades.

Sheldon should have taken the four steps of rapport by design to "connect" with his customer: 1) adopting a Really Useful Attitude to lead her toward his goal; 2) synchronizing her body language and voice tone during their conversation; 3) using open questions and actively listening to her responses; and 4) picking up on her sensory preferences along the way.

you will be able to communicate with him or her on a more appropriate wavelength, be it Visual, Auditory or Kinesthetic.

In this way, you will be hours—sometimes years—ahead of where you would have been if you had not known how to figure out an individual's sensory preference.

Developing a knack for detecting sensory preferences means paying close attention to others—and this alone makes you more people oriented.

On the next pages you will find four quick, written exercises that will help you consolidate your learning. Photocopy these pages or just write in the book. Fill in what you can without referring back to this chapter or to the chapter before it.

Auditories will want to talk their way through these exercises and tell themselves the answers, and Visuals will want to picture the answers in their head, but the answers must be written down. Writing down the answers will oblige you to use all three senses—and that's the quickest way to incorporate this information into your memory and your life skills.

After you've filled in as much as you can, flip back over the previous pages to add to your answers.

Physically, how do they look different?

Visual	Auditory	Kinesthetic

How do they sound different?		
Visual	Auditory	Kinesthetic

How do they dress differently?		
Visual	Auditory	Kinesthetic

What gifts would you buy for them?

Visual	Auditory	Kinesthetic

The foregoing "clues" in spotting sensory preferences are generalizations, of course. But when several of these generalizations point in the same direction, the chances are pretty good that you have discovered the primary way a person perceives the world. This will be your most effective tool in establishing rapport and connecting with others.

Putting It All Together

People are drawn to one another and are eager to connect—to be liked.

Successful communicators don't go out into the world every day loaded up with skills and techniques; they go out and take what they do for granted. It's in the "letting go" that the people, things and events in your life flow easily. This is the difference between those who struggle and get nowhere, and those who appear to do very little and have everything.

The more you act upon what you have learned here, the more you will effortlessly just assume rapport with other people. Of course, you must practice, but soon it will be as natural as riding a bike or swimming— two other skills you mastered only on the day you let go of worrying and had faith.

This book is about connecting with your greatest resource: other people. It's about establishing rapport, an instant bond, with them as you join together mentally. You have seen that rapport is the link between meeting and communicating, and how the quality and depth of the rapport you establish can affect your outcome. Rapport can happen naturally or by design.

We have looked at the meaning of communication as the response you get and how, in order for your communication to achieve its desired outcome, a little KFC can go a long way—in fact, not just in communication but in all areas of your life where you want a positive result.

The basic template for greeting someone new is: Open—Eye—Beam—"Hi!"—Lean. You are first with the open body language, eye contact, smile and "Hi," and the lean sets you up for synchronizing. You can remember that when you point your heart at another person you convey your openness.

You can choose your attitude. A Really Useful Attitude is paramount to how others perceive you and how you feel about yourself. You know that your attitude keeps you congruent, or believable, according to the three "V's" of communication. In other words, when you have a Really *Useless* Attitude like anger, you look angry, sound angry and use angry words—all unappealing. Conversely, it's easy to make yourself likable when you adopt a Really *Useful* Attitude, let's say, welcoming, because you will look welcoming, sound welcoming and use welcoming words.

We have covered body language, open and closed, and seen how, along with facial expressions and gestures, it makes up slightly more than half of what other people get from us. That's why it is so valuable in synchronizing for rapport by design.

When we say "I like you" to someone, what we really mean is "I am like you." In rapport by design, we don't wait hopefully to see if we have things in common; we move straight into synchronizing the body language, voice tone and words of the person we are meeting. We know that we have unconsciously been synchronizing emotional feedback all our lives from the people who have influenced us—parents, peers, teachers, and so on—and therefore it's easy and natural to synchronize other people in order to make them feel comfortable with us.

In terms of talking with a new acquaintance, we have seen that questions are the generators of conversation and that they fall into two categories: open and closed. Open questions open people up, and that's the goal of conversation. You know that giving physical and spoken feedback will "keep the ball in play." Conversation is about describing your experiences to others, and the more colorfully you can do it, the more you can "talk in color," the better they can imagine and share your experiences—and as a consequence increase the bonding and rapport you are creating by design.

You have learned, to your surprise and delight, that every person you meet or already know presents you with a sensory puzzle. Do they prefer to connect on a Visual, Auditory or Kinesthetic wavelength? You have begun developing insight into their perceptions of the world around them.

In fact, even if you have begun to implement the techniques in this book and gotten it all wrong—you are still getting it right! You are being proactive with people, as opposed to reactive or passive. There is no downside; you can't lose. If you are carefully observing people's body language and expressions, listening to their words, watching their eye movements, giving feedback and making conversation—you are being proactive and they can't help but like you. As long as you have a Really Useful Attitude.

Where Do I Start?

Let me reiterate that this is not a new way of being, not a new way of life. I haven't given you a magic wand to rush out into the street with and start tapping people over the head to make them like you. These are tools and techniques that help you establish rapport quickly.

We have covered the four basic areas of making people like you in 90 seconds or less: attitude, synchronization, conversation and sensory preferences. Improvement in any one of these areas will increase your ability to communicate effectively and quickly with other people. As you learn to incorporate all four stages into your face-to-face encounters, the effects will become more and more apparent.

You know why you connect naturally with some people and not with others, and since starting the book you have probably already begun to improve your relationships at home and at work. You are approaching people with increased confidence and sincerity and enjoying each new experience. And you have realized that you already possess most of the skills needed for making natural connections with other people.

The more you use the many tools we have shared throughout this entire book—from the image you project with a Really Useful Attitude to the sincerity and charisma you impart in your greeting, from the comfort and empathy generated by synchronizing to the ability to recognize which sense a person most relies upon— the more you'll be able to establish rapport with ease and make people like you in 90 seconds or less.

If I had to assign a priority to these four aspects, a Really Useful Attitude stands alone in its power to generate good feelings in yourself and in others. Attitude is infectious and obvious, and it precedes you. Your attitude not only drives your behavior, it drives the behavior of others—and comes across in your body language, your voice tone and the words you use. You will notice an immediate improvement in your rapport skills the moment you begin to manage your attitude. On the flip side, if not properly managed, your attitude will work against you—just as fast. Attitude can attract or repel.

Next, without doubt, is the amazing power of synchronizing. As you have seen, synchronization is part of our natural makeup, and it's what we already do unconsciously with those people we like. When you meet someone and you want to establish quick rapport, start synchronizing immediately. It will feel odd at first unless you've done the exercise on synchronizing in groups of three (see page 82), in which case you'll wonder how you ever got along without it. Two or three days are ample to become proficient, even brilliant, in this department. After all, you've been doing it your whole life, in one way or another, with the people who are close to you.

As your conversation skills improve and you encourage the other person to do plenty of talking, you will find yourself having time to make observations about sensory preferences. Let this come gently. Do you remember those Magic-Eye books from the early '90s? You'd gaze at some weird-looking picture and slowly, eventually, your eyes would refocus and you'd see a picture in 3-D. Discovering sensory preferences is like that. You look and you search, and you get frustrated, and then suddenly you refocus on people and they start to look different as you establish an elegant, deep rapport at the subconscious level, where true unity is achieved. The unfolding and detection of someone's sensory preference will continue after your 90 seconds and give you the vehicle to travel much deeper into rapport by design with your new person—your newest great resource.

So, you're at a conference and you've just met Sylvie Clairoux, the head of the department you'd like to work for. The connecting is smooth, warm, sincere and respectful; your Really Useful Attitude and openness made for a perfect "greeting." Although there are seven people at the meeting, you synchronize her body movements but with no excess eye contact. Her subconscious picks it up. There is chance eye contact, she smiles politely, you acknowledge—BINGO! You've been practicing this daily and have easily realized by her dress, her voice, her choice of words, eye movements and tonality that she's probably Auditory. When you speak, you synchronize her voice tone and use Auditory words ("That sounds great!" . . . "Everybody on the team has voiced an opinion."). How can this stranger not like you when you look, sound and move so much like her? At the break, you get her to one side.

"I'd like to hear more about the proposal," you begin.

"Haven't we met before?" Ms. Clairoux asks.

"I think she likes you!" whispers the little voice in your head.

Assuming Rapport

As I write this book, I assume I like you, the reader. I assume I need you; I assume you need me. And what's more, I assume I'm right. This is what gives me the confidence to keep on writing. We need each other; that's the real basis for our rapport. And here we are connecting.

We can harness the power of imagination to make useful assumptions. We receive so much information from our five senses that we can't possibly process it all consciously. Instead it gets sorted into three separate lots. The main batch of information you *delete* from your consciousness. For example, you weren't aware of your left foot until I just drew your attention to it, and you probably haven't got a clue how your fingernails grow. The second batch you *distort*; you feed it into your imagination and play around with it, imagining your upcoming vacation, getting paranoid about the battery in your smoke detector, that sort of thing. And the third batch is stored away under the heading of *generalizations,* or assumptions. When you've seen one frying pan, you can make an assumption that the big metal thing on your neighbor's stove with the long handle and the sizzling pancakes in it is a frying pan; you don't have to find out all over again what it is. Your brain will make a generalized assumption.

Assumptions at their best are great for learning, but at their worst they lead to biased, unfair, limiting and dangerous fantasies. If your imagination has been distorting information to scare you away from people, all I ask is your understanding that your imagination is tricking you into making negative assumptions about people based on past experience. In this case, your imagination is running the show and the score is Imagination one, You zero.

Get your imagination under control. See it for the fun vehicle it is and use it to install some Really Useful Assumptions. Here are a few to get you going. After reading them, close your eyes and see what they will look, sound and feel like:

Assume rapport and trust between yourself and other people.

Assume/trust that you will like them and that they will like you.

Assume that what you'll be doing with other people—connecting, synchronizing, etc.—will work.

Assume that others will give you the benefit of the doubt, and you will do the same for them.

Assume that what you've learned from this book will work for you because it's worked for thousands of other people.

Assume that you are making a difference in the lives of the individuals you meet.

Assume that this difference is for the better, not just in their lives but also in your community as a whole.

Assume that a connected community is a place where we encourage, uplift and promote each other.

People who connect live longer; people who connect get cooperation; and people who connect feel safe and strong. People who connect evolve. Together we rise and fall, together we sink or swim, together we laugh and cry. And when all is said and done, it's people that make the hard times bearable and the good times much, much sweeter.

A Modern-Day Parable

L ately I've been giving a lot of talks to high school students. Many of them are looking for part-time or summer employment, and they need to sharpen their job-seeking and people skills. I'll never forget one particular student who sullenly interrupted my talk.

"Hey, man, I've gone to lots of job interviews and they never hire me," he griped. "I tried at a grocery store, a drugstore, an office . . . "

Other students around him began to snicker. The reason was pretty clear. The young man was wearing torn army pants and a T-shirt with the word "Rancid" splashed across the front (that's the name of a thrash-punk band). His left ear was pierced in three places and he had a nose ring, too. Even more to the point, he sported a bright green Mohawk that stood up six inches high on his otherwise shaved head.

"What do you want?" I asked him.

"A job, whaddya think?"

"Have you thought of changing what you're doing to get it?"

He glared at me, his arms crossed tightly over his chest. "Changing what?"

"How about the way you look?" I asked, leaning forward.

"No way, man!" he practically hollered. "If they don't like how I look, that's discrimination!"

"Look, I see your point," I said. (He was Visual.) "But we both know how the world works. So what do you want? The job or the haircut?"

There was a long silence. Finally he uncrossed his arms and rolled his eyeballs upward. "The job, I guess," he muttered. Some of the other students laughed good-naturedly. Slowly, he began to laugh, too. Then we all laughed. That's what it's all about.

.

The Small Things That Make a Big Difference Workbook

Appendix

 **Workbook**

First Things First

There's only so much you can learn about riding a horse by reading a book. Sooner or later you're going to have to climb up into the saddle. At first all that wobbling around might feel silly and unnatural, but before you know it, with a little practice, horseback riding becomes natural and easy. The same goes for connecting with people. At first it might seem awkward and embarrassing to approach people you don't know, or don't know very well, and assume rapport with them. With a little practice, though, it soon becomes second nature. And so it should. After all, you were born with everything you need to connect and communicate with others: a body, a voice, five senses and what I call "Super Powers," namely enthusiasm, curiosity, the ability to process feedback, empathy and imagination. In face-to-face communication, as in horseback riding, baking, game playing, rocket science, you name it, it's almost always the small things that make the big differences.

You might be saying to yourself, "Fine, I buy all that,

and I've read the book. But how do I actually practice making people like me?" The answer's right here: 21 small, simple exercises to fine-tune your natural-born abilities to connect with other people, not just for friendship but for success at school, work, everywhere. They'll even help you find a loving relationship, if that's what you're after.

Many of the exercises in this little workbook can be grasped in 90 seconds or less. To get the most out of them, it's important to remember the golden rule: There is no such thing as failure, there is only feedback.

The key is to process the feedback you receive, and use it to do better next time. All human behavior is a feedback loop. Try something. If it doesn't work, learn from it, change your tactic, and try again.

A pilot doesn't take off from London and aim her plane at Miami and leave it at that. She evaluates her course, the weather and other air traffic, and makes corrections along the way. She continually processes feedback and makes adjustments until she gets to her desired destination. If she didn't, the plane could end up in the Atlantic Ocean or the Sahara Desert! The same thing goes for the exercises in this workbook. Try them out, see how they go and make corrections until they work for you.

This workbook is not about becoming someone you are not; it's about making the most of what you've got and being yourself. You were born with what it takes. You'll get there with practice and feedback. You can do it—there's no question about it.

1. Before You Begin

I f your heart's not really in it, these simple exercises aren't going to work for you. So, let's start by taking stock of your commitment so we can get some leverage on your determination.

On a scale of 1 to 10, with 10 being the strongest:

How engaged are you prepared to be with these exercises?

   1   2   3   4   5   6   7   8   9   10

How much risk are you prepared to take?

   1   2   3   4   5   6   7   8   9   10

How great is your desire to connect with new people?

   1   2   3   4   5   6   7   8   9   10

Total your score. If it is less than 15, either your heart's not really in it or your lack of self-confidence is getting you down. This book's preface begins with a simple quotation: "The 'secret' of success is not very hard to figure out. The better you are at connecting with other people, the better the quality of your life." No matter how old you are, when you are open and able to connect easily and quickly with others, you will flourish. It has nothing to do with brains, beauty or talent and everything to do with your enthusiasm for getting cooperation from others. Tell yourself to put that enthusiasm to work right here, starting with the next exercise, and carry it on through to the very last one.

2. Who Do You Want to Connect With?

Picture your life. What do you want it to be like in, say, a year's time? Dare to dream a little. Gather together a bunch of magazines (used is fine). At least a few should be magazines you wouldn't normally read. Cut out pictures, words, bits of advertisements—anything you see that relates to your image—and put them together in a collage that creates a picture of your life as you want it to be. Create images that are as specific and concrete as you can. You can write or draw on it if you like. Put it on a wall or someplace where you can see it every day.

The next step helps it work much better: explain to a friend or family member (or even your pet will do) what your collage means. What's important is hearing yourself describe out loud the life you want. Seeing and hearing your dream will make it more real in your mind.

With your collage in front of you, think about the types of people you'll need to connect with to make your dream happen. Who are they? Make a list of people (specific individuals and/or a type of person) for each of the categories below:

Colleagues

_____

_____

Friends or potential friends

_____

_____

Association or club members

_____

_____

Neighbors

_____

_____

Parents of children your children play with

_____

_____

Friends or relatives you aren't close
to but would like to know better

_____

_____

Others

_____

_____

_____

_____

3. Your Comfort Level When Meeting People

Using a scale of 1 to 10 with 10 being the strongest, answer the questions below in the context of meeting someone new at school or work and in a social setting:

	School/ Work	Social Setting
How comfortable do you feel?		
How friendly are you?		
How easily do you make eye contact?		
How easy is it for you to get someone talking to you?		
How often do you remember the person's name?		
How good are you at finding common ground?		

If there is a difference in your comfort level at work and in social situations, why do you think that is? What are some things you could do to increase your comfort level in different settings?

4. My Really Useful Attitude

First impressions can be lasting impressions. The first impression people get from you doesn't stem from what you're wearing or how you've done your hair, it comes from your attitude. Take a look again at the lists of Really Useful and Really Useless Attitudes on page 41, then answer the following questions:

1. What is the ideal me that I would like everyone to see?

_____

_____

2. What kind of attitudes can I adopt to present the best possible me?

_____

_____

3. What are some specific ways I can convey my best attitude(s) when meeting people?

_____

_____

During the next week, be on the lookout for people you come across who seem appealing to you. Analyze their behavior and answer the following questions:

1. What was their attitude?

_____

_____

2. What specifically did they do or say that gave you that first impression?

_____

_____

3. Did being around them make you feel somewhat the same way?

_____

_____

Now, think back to a time recently when you felt enthusiastic.

1. What was responsible for your enthusiasm?

_____

_____

2. Do you think you displayed your enthusiasm in a way that other people picked up on?

_____

_____

3. How can you link how you felt at that time to yourself and your approach to finishing every single exercise in this book—in order?

_____

_____

4. How can you convey your enthusiasm to others during conversations?

_____

_____

5. What attitude or combination of attitudes would you like to show when you meet someone new?

_____

_____

5. Chance Encounters

Read the following scenarios. Using the details of the situation, decide what you would say. Come up with a conversational statement or two for each, and then follow it with an open question. For example, if you found yourself waiting in a huge line at an airport to reschedule your flight, which was canceled because of stormy weather, you might say to your neighbors, "Man, this line is long!" Then ask, "Have you heard a recent weather forecast?" or, "I'm glad I'm not the clerk doing all that reticketing—can you imagine dealing with so many frustrated people?"

1. It's raining, and as you leave the store, several people are waiting under the awning for the rain to let up. Like you, they have no umbrellas. You are standing near someone and you say _____

_____

_____.

2. You're at work, and you go to the lounge for a cup of coffee. You notice someone you don't know, who works in another department. You approach and say _____

_____

_____.

3. On your way to class, you stop at a convenience store for a snack and notice someone you've seen around campus perusing the chip offerings. You say _____

_____

_____.

6. The Three-Second Rule

Did you ever miss an opportunity because you deliberated about it so long that the chance passed? Or talk yourself out of doing something and then regret it later? Have you ever sat in a café nursing a cold latté watching other people enjoy themselves while you never budged or made a move? "I'll just order another latté, then I'll go for it and strike up a conversation." "Next time he looks this way, I'll smile at him." If you just hang around wishing, waiting and hoping for something to happen, nothing ever will. Then you end up feeling bad because you talked yourself out of something or just plain chickened out. The longer you wait, the more reason you have to beat yourself up for procrastinating.

Sometimes we just have to go for it. The more you practice, the easier it gets.

Over the course of a week, approach three new people every day and say something simple.

Spot a person you're interested in, count to three, and on three go up and speak to him or her. If you hesitate, you lose. So zoom right in. You are creating a new habit, with "one, two, three" as your trigger. Practice, practice, practice—just do it. The worst that can happen is that you put a dent in your ego. The best is that you make a new connection. Assume the best.

Your goal here is not to start a conversation. The purpose of this exercise is to eliminate hesitation and self-censorship. The important thing is that you make your way over to the people the moment you spot them. You'll say, "One, two, three" in your head, and go without hesitation. This will help you create a new habit. Here are a few examples of simple openers you could use:

> "Excuse me, which end of the mall is closer to the train station?"
>
> "Hi. Can you tell me where I can get a good cup of coffee near here?"
>
> "Pardon me, do you know what time it is?"

Remember that the first move is just as important as the first impression. So practice, practice, practice, until you feel comfortable—and then keep on doing it.

7. Me Too— Finding Common Ground

At the heart of establishing instant rapport is the hunt for common ground, and one of the best ways to find it is to look for "Me too" moments (see page 68). Simply pay attention to what's being said, and when the opportunity arises, jump in and say it— as long as it's true. For example, if someone says, "I love the Caribbean," you can simply say, "Me too!" However, don't just keep repeating "Me too." Mix it up by using phrases like "Wow, what a coincidence," "No kidding, I totally agree" and "I love it there too." And of course you can add to the conversation by asking follow-up questions; for instance, "What's your favorite island?" and "Do you snorkel?"

During your next three conversations with people you don't

know particularly well (in other words, not your best friend or mother!), make an effort to find "Me too" moments.

For each conversation, what was the first thing you were able to find in common?

Conversation 1 _____

Conversation 2 _____

Conversation 3 _____

1. **Did you feel that these moments changed the feeling of the conversation?** _____

_____

2. **Did you feel a stronger connection to the person?** _____

_____

3. **Did the person respond differently to you?** _____

_____

4. **Did the conversation come more easily?** _____

_____

8. Know What You Want in the Positive

Take each of the following statements and turn it from a negative take on what you *don't* want to a positive approach to what you *do* want:

Don't leave home without an umbrella. _____

_____

Don't miss your train. _____

_____

Don't be shy. _____

_____

Don't forget to lock your bike. _____

_____

Don't forget to give me a call._____

_____

Don't worry. _____

_____

Don't leave the lights on when you depart. _____

_____

9. Making Eye Contact

When you meet someone new, it's important to be able to look him or her in the eye. This exercise will help you practice that skill and, hopefully, set you on the path to establishing rapport.

The next time you greet three new people or people you don't know well (for example, the person behind the deli counter; a person you often see in your elevator at work), keep the following questions in mind, then write down the answers as soon as you get a chance.

Were you able to make eye contact?

_____

What color were their eyes?

_____

Did you say hello?

_____

How did they respond to you?

_____

Did you feel you were able to establish rapport with them?

_____

Did you learn their names? What are they?

_____

10. Great, Great, Great

Not everyone has an easy, natural smile, so here's a simple trick that fashion models use. They keep saying the word "great"—after a few seconds it makes a person's eyes smile.

Look into a mirror and say "great" over and over, each time using a different, crazy tone of voice until you crack up. Say it loud, whisper it, say it in a laid-back voice, in a sexy voice. It will not only make you smile, it will also make you feel good. It's simply that it's a very positive word. (It also has that "ay" syllable in the middle that requires you to bare your top teeth in a kind of smile during the process.)

For one day, every time you meet someone, smile. If you have trouble, say "great" to yourself three times before you approach the person. You'll be smiling by the time you get there.

11. Heart to Heart

For the next few days, be observant of people's body language and see how it affects you. Do your best to keep your body language open and relaxed. When you meet someone new, point your heart warmly at the person's heart. Rather than crossing your arms over your chest, keep your heart open, signaling that you don't mean any harm.

Practice opening and closing your body language when you are talking with someone and notice the difference in your attitude as well as the response. Get into the habit of using open body language when you are seeking cooperation from others.

12. Synchronizing

The next time you are talking with someone, synchronize your body language with his or hers for 30 seconds (for a refresher on synchronizing, see page 69). Take a break for 30 seconds and then synchronize again. Did you notice a difference between the synchronized and unsynchronized period? Did people respond positively when you were synchronized?

13. Closed to Open

Read the following closed questions, then change each one into an open question—one that begins with who, why, what, when, where or how.

1. **Have you thought about my suggestions?**

_____

_____

2. Are you interested in the Buy One, Get One Free promotion we have going on right now?

_____

_____

3. Do you want to go out for dinner sometime?

_____

_____

4. Have you taken the finance course already?

_____

_____

5. Have you thought about how you're going to market yourself in the interview?

_____

_____

Sometimes a closed question is unavoidable. The key in this situation is to quickly follow it with an open question. For instance, if you ask, "Do you live in the neighborhood?" and the person replies, "Yes," you should continue the conversation by following up with an open question, such as "How do you like it?"

Write an open question that you could use to follow each closed question below:

1. Is this the right track for the 7:15 train into the city?

_____

_____

2. Can I help you find something?

_____

_____

3. Have you signed up to volunteer yet?

_____

_____

14. Conversation Starters

Questions beginning with "Are you," "Did you" and "Have you" often get a yes or no answer and don't encourage dialogue. But questions that begin with *Who*, *What*, *Why*, *Where*, *When* or *How* tend to open people up and get them talking. Come up with three open questions that you could ask new people in each of the following situations:

Before a meeting

_____

_____

_____

At a party

_____

_____

_____

Waiting for a bus or train

_____

_____

_____

In line before a movie

_____

_____

_____

The best open question isn't even a question. Try starting a conversation with "Tell me about . . ."

15. Making Yourself Memorable

What good is meeting someone for the first time, creating a favorable impression and establishing rapport if two weeks later the person has forgotten you?

1. List three people you've met who have "trademark" looks and describe the qualities that make them memorable.

_____   _____   _____

_____   _____   _____

_____   _____   _____

2. What are things about you that your friends comment on? (Do you have great hair, do you wear bold colors, have a great voice? Are you short or tall?)

_____

_____

3. What is the signature style or persona you picture for yourself?

_____

_____

4. What aspect of your current self could you emphasize to create a "trademark" look?

_____

_____

5. Is there something new that you could adopt and make your signature (e.g., wearing a brightly colored scarf or stylish eyeglasses)?

_____

_____

6. What concrete steps do you need to take to achieve this memorable persona or style?

_____

_____

16. Sensory Preferences

Everybody has a primary sense that they use to perceive the world. Some people respond to the world and make their decisions based mostly on how things look (Visual), others by how things sound (Auditory) and others by physical sensation or how they feel (Kinesthetic). Imagine being able to know which sense somebody relies on most. When you find out, you can appeal to that sense above all others. The other person won't realize why, but he or she will feel drawn to you.

Visual, Auditory and Kinesthetic groups of people are very different from each other. They think differently. They want different things, have different desires, have differing motivations; they speak and dress differently.

When you can find out the sensory preference of the people in your life you will communicate at a much deeper level.

To practice identifying Visual, Auditory and Kinesthetic types of people, read each phrase and fill in the blank to the right with the type of person who would say it.

We all have differing viewpoints.	
Can you grasp the basics?	
That sounds like a great idea.	
Show me how you did it.	
I hear you loud and clear.	
I see what you're saying.	
We're up against the wall.	
Can you shed some light on this problem?	
That name rings a bell.	
I can't put my finger on anything concrete.	
Are you tuning in to what she's saying?	
Let's explore a little deeper.	

17. Sensory Identification

Think of three people you know well—for example, your best friend, your spouse, a coworker—and put their names in the spaces below. Try to recall discussions you've had with them and see if you can determine what their dominant approach is.

	Person 1	Person 2	Person 3
Name			
Favorite words or phrases			
Pace of their speech			
The way they dress			
The direction of their gaze when they are thinking			
Are they big-picture or detail oriented?			
Do they like lots of auditory stimulation or peace and quiet?			
Do you think they are Visual, Auditory, or Kinesthetic?			

18. Talking Sense

Close your eyes and imagine you are at a busy airport with an hour to spare before your flight. Using the chart below, write down all the things you can see, hear, touch, taste, and smell.

Once you have made your list, take 30 seconds to describe to yourself in sharp detail what you see. Then take another 30 seconds to do the same for what you hear, then for what you feel, smell and taste.

Which of the senses came most easily and which was most difficult?

When you can figure out the primary sense of the people you know and meet, you can communicate with them more effectively on their own wavelength. If they think in pictures, talk to them in images, or at least talk about how things look. If they favor sounds, tell them how things sound. And if they are concerned with physical sensation, tell them how things feel.

To see this in action, go back and reread the story of "Ingrid's Hard-Earned Vacation" on page 152.

See	Hear	Touch	Taste	Smell

See	Hear	Touch	Taste	Smell

19. Appeal to the Senses

To practice speaking to different types of people, describe each of the following items first using Visual words, then using Auditory and finally using Kinesthetic words. (If you need help, check out the word lists on pages 140–145.)

Your dream house

_____

_____

_____

Your dream vacation

_____

_____

_____

Your favorite meal

_____

_____

_____

20. Talking in Color

Conversation often entails describing your experiences to others. The more senses you involve in your descriptions, the more interesting people will find you and the better they will remember you and what you say.

This exercise works better with a partner who can respond to you. If you don't have anyone to do this with, write your answers down.

Describing sights, sounds, touch, smells, and tastes,

Talk about how patience feels.

_____

_____

Talk about your most cherished possession.

_____

_____

Talk about winter.

_____

_____

Talk about one of the promises you keep making to yourself.

_____

_____

Talk about the things you do to entertain yourself.

_____

_____

The point of this exercise is to get away from talking in facts and figures because they fade fast and are boring. Mental images are worth a thousand words; they trigger emotions and stick in the mind.

21. Putting It All Together—The Get-Involved Action Plan

It sounds obvious, but you have to get out and meet people before you can make friends with them. You're not going to make friends with everyone you meet, but the more activities you participate in, the more places you visit, the sooner you'll make new friends and acquaintances.

There are dozens of ways to get your foot in the door of places where people get together. This plan will help you figure out a plan of attack for getting involved and socializing.

1. **What type of group are you most interested in joining?**
>   **Sports (leagues/yoga/gym/snowboarding)**
>   **Cultural interests (music/books/film)**
>   **Volunteering/outreach**
>   **Classes (cooking/languages/crafts/spot-welding/yoga/pottery)**
>   **Religious organizations**

2. What is one thing you've always wanted to do? Go hot-air ballooning; drive a cab; learn Flamenco dancing; become a bullfighter, a synchronized swimmer; build a tree house. Write down something you'd really like to try.

_____

_____

3. What could be a first step to achieving that goal? Is it looking online or in the yellow pages and making a call? Asking a friend or a local organization?

_____

_____

4. Make yourself take the first step, and the rest will follow more easily.

A Final Thought:
There Is No Rejection,
Only Selection

As you go out and start meeting new people, one final thing that can make a big difference for the worse—if you let it—is the way you handle rejection. I had more than my share of rejection when I was growing up, and I learned the hard way that there are essentially three things you can do with rejection: you can dismiss it, you can let it get to you and wreak havoc with your self-confidence or you can welcome it.

What are you going to do when you are rejected? It's bound to happen sometime; it's part of life. Handling rejection requires an immediate adjustment in attitude. If a person doesn't return your interest, that's not a cue to give up and get depressed, it's a call to move on! If you were an apple picker and you came upon a tree without apples on its branches, would you take it personally and feel hurt and sorry for yourself? Of course not! You'd just admit there was nothing there for you and move on to the next tree. If you feel sorry for yourself, you've lost sight of your goal.

Most people will let you know they're not interested in friendship in a diplomatic way, but you'll probably meet some rude and ungracious characters along the way too. When you do, just excuse yourself politely and give thanks that you found out what kind of person he or she was relatively quickly, before you invested more of your time and emotions in this "relationship." Ideally, the rejection/selection process would be painless, but you'll probably get your feelings bruised once or twice. It's human nature to feel bad in situations like this, but don't let yourself wallow. Instead, you have to welcome rejection/selection as part of the exploration, the journey, the adventure.

Understanding the principle that there's no rejection, only selection, means that if you're chatting with someone and things aren't clicking, it's not anybody's fault. It has nothing to do with you as an individual. It just means you don't have enough in common or you're not psychologically compatible. So, enjoy your time together, be yourself, remain polite and gracious. At the end say thanks and good-bye and move on. And remember, you may end up doing some rejection (politely and diplomatically as well, of course) yourself: you don't have to try to be lifelong friends with everyone you meet.

In closing, my wish for you is simple. If you're reading this book, one of your priorities is to connect with people. Don't ignore this important part of your life! You have to make time. Set aside at least 15 minutes a day to get out and practice, practice, practice these exercises. Sure, you might find it difficult at first, but keep at it. Try one or two a day until they become second nature. Turn off the TV, the computer, the PlayStation, set aside your work and dedicate your time for the next three weeks to working your way through all the exercises. Nobody—except you—even has to know you're doing them. Don't try too hard, be yourself and place this phrase on the tip of your tongue: "There is no such thing as failure, there is only feedback."

About the Author

Nicholas Boothman has been called "one of the leading experts in face-to-face communication in the world" by John Tierney at *The New York Times*, and *The Economist* magazine's Matthew Bishop found him "truly inspirational."

Nicholas spent more than two decades studying the ways in which human beings connect, communicate and collaborate, and has taught his revolutionary technique of "Fully Connected Communication" to corporations, colleges and universities around the world, including both the Harvard and London business schools. His corporate certification programs are delivered by licensed trainers in North America, Europe, Asia and Africa, and his Connect90 and TeenConnect90 programs, along with their social networking websites, connect90.com and teenconnect90.com, teach interactive, face-to-face people skills and boost self-confidence.

A former fashion and advertising photographer who dealt with hundreds of new faces a week for clients like AT&T, Revlon and Coca-Cola, he is now a world-renowned expert in turning first impressions into lasting relationships.

.